# Touring The

# *PUEBLOS*

A travel guide which takes the visitor to all 20 living Pueblo Indian reservations in New Mexico and Arizona

**RON SWARTLEY**

Frontier Image Press

Copyright ©Ron Swartley 1993
All rights reserved. No part of this book
may be reproduced or transmitted
in any form or by any means,
electronic or mechanical, including
photocopying, recording, or by any
information storage and retrieval
system without permission from
the publisher.

Library of Congress Catalog Number 93-070277

ISBN 0-9634309-1-2

Frontier Image Press
P.O. Box 8040
Albuquerque NM 87198

TO
**DR. ROSS WOODRUFF**
Who introduced me to
Native Americana

COVER PHOTO: ACOMA "SKY CITY" SCENE

# CONTENTS

IN THE BEGINNING ... 9

ABOUT YOUR VISIT ... 15

## PART ONE -- EIGHT NORTHERN PUEBLOS

TAOS ... 23

PICURIS ... 31

SAN JUAN ... 37

SANTA CLARA ... 43

SAN ILDEFONSO ... 49

NAMBE ... 55

POJOAQUE, SANTA ANA ... 61

TESUQUE ... 67

## PART TWO -- MIDDLE RIO GRANDE PUEBLOS

COCHITI ... 73

SANTO DOMINGO ... 79

SAN FELIPE ... 85

ZIA ... 91

JEMEZ ... 95

SANDIA ... 101

ISLETA ... 107

## PART THREE – WESTERN PUEBLOS

LAGUNA ............................................................. 113

ACOMA 'SKY CITY' ........................................... 119

ZUNI .................................................................. 127

HOPI .................................................................. 135

## APPENDICES

INDIAN PUEBLO CULTURAL CENTER ............... 147

HOW TO BUY INDIAN ARTS AND CRAFTS ........ 149

PUEBLO TOURIST ATTRACTIONS ..................... 155

**INDEX** ............................................................. 157

## MAPS

THE PUEBLO WORLD ......................................... 8

EIGHT NORTHERN PUEBLOS ............................ 22

MIDDLE RIO GRANDE PUEBLOS ....................... 72

WESTERN PUEBLOS .......................................... 112

HOPI VILLAGES .................................................. 134

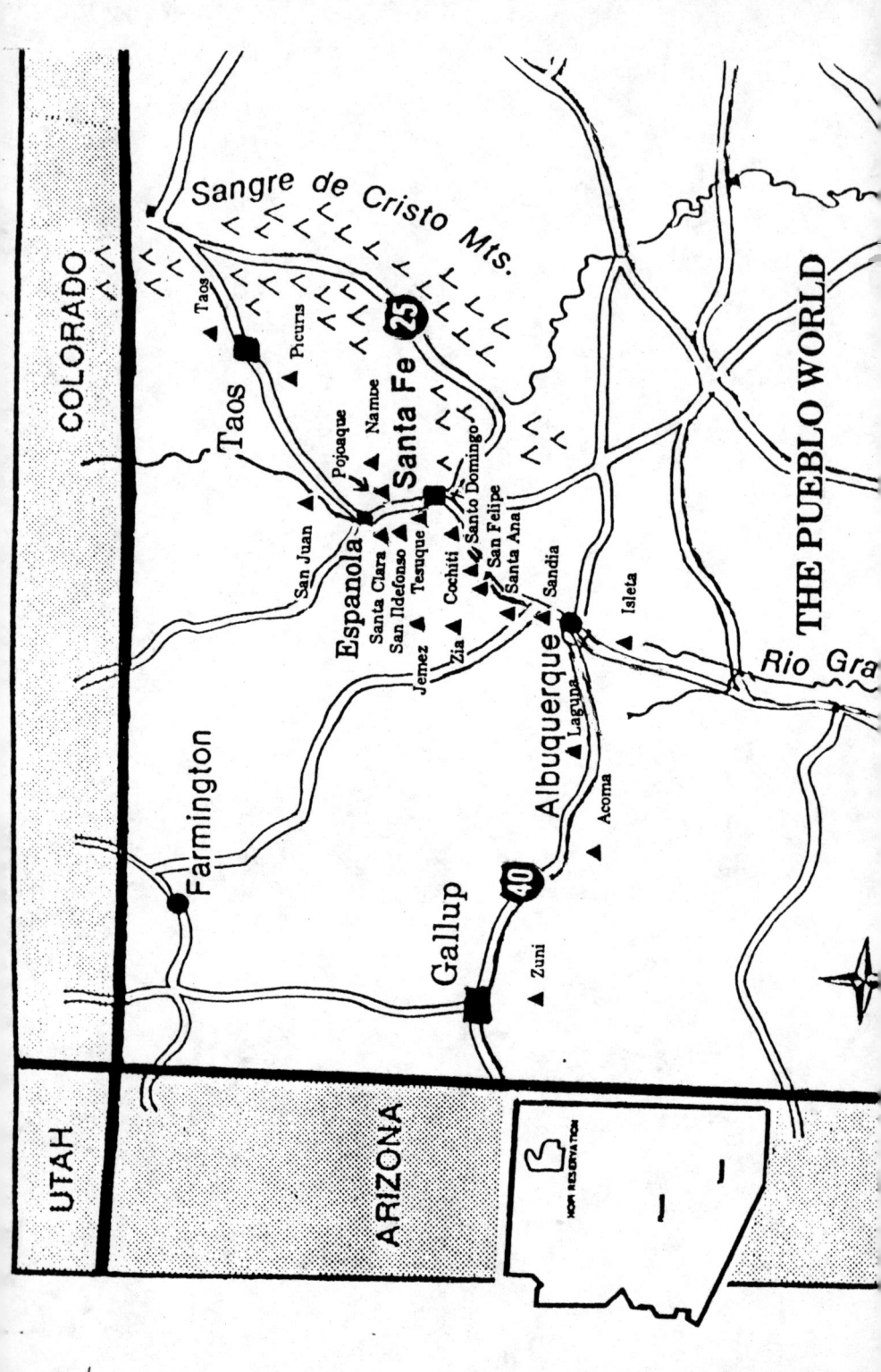

# IN THE BEGINNING

At the height of the Pueblo Indian civilization in the American Southwest, well before the first arrival of Europeans in 1539, there were literally thousands of villages, with a population numbering in the tens of thousands. Today there are only about 30 of the original villages left, on 20 small reservations, with most counting only a few hundred residents. A small minority of these pueblos has become so assimilated by the engulfing mainstream that they've lost much of their tribal identity. But the majority have stubbornly hung onto significant vestiges of the "old ways" of speaking, worshiping and making a living. They're unique nations within a nation, providing an enlightening and colorful contrast with a powerful mainstream culture which stresses modernity and change. A visit to a pueblo's ancient dusty streets can't help but provide a glimpse of a dim North American past, when dwellings were made of layered rock and covered with mud, when bread was baked in outdoor ovens, when pottery was used for storage, transport and cooking, and when life's routines were centered around

*Touring The Pueblos*

the fundamental need of survival in an often hostile environment.

A tour of the Indian pueblos - 19 in New Mexico, one in Arizona - is a trip taken into a primitive past; a visit to a living museum, where many of the "artifacts" are not only on display, but in daily use.

Such a visit might well start with the northernmost village - *Taos* - 70 miles north of Santa Fe. The magnificent, multi-story communal "apartment buildings" of this pueblo have existed for at least 600 years.

Your travels would take you south a few miles to the *Picuris Pueblo*, where artisans continue to make age-old micaceous pottery. Continuing further south you'll come on the *San Juan Pueblo* - a center of tribal government — and the *Santa Clara Pueblo*, with its impressive Puye Cliff Dwellings. Nearby is the *San Ildefonso Pueblo* with its world famous black-on-black pottery. Further south still, not far from the meandering Rio Grande but still in New Mexico's northern high country, are the pueblos of *Tesuque, Nambe* and *Pojoaque*. The land drops off to lower, flatter desert then, the Rio Grande flowing out from between high cliffs into Cochiti Lake, below which is the *Cochiti Pueblo*, noted for its famed storyteller figures. Further down the river is the *Santo Domingo* tribe, long famous for its heishe necklaces; and the *San Felipe* tribe, long famous for the quality and pageantry of its ceremonial dances. The next three pueblos — *Santa Ana, Zia* and *Jemez* - depart a bit from the Rio Grande, to be located north along the Jemez, where the earth turns red and the cliffs spectacular. Back along the Rio Grande and further south still are the two remaining Rio Grande pueblos, *Sandia* on the north edge of Albuquerque, and *Isleta* just

*In The Beginning*

to the south.

The visitor to Puebloland must turn west to reach the remaining four villages. *Old Laguna Pueblo* - the last one established - is 47 miles west of Albuquerque, along a busy Interstate. *Acoma Pueblo*, with its famous "Sky City" is just a few miles southwest of Laguna. The *Zuni Pueblo* - the first one visited by Spanish explorers back in 1540 - is about 70 miles further west and a bit south. Finally there are the *Hopi Pueblo* villages - the only pueblo complex outside New Mexico - about 100 miles northwest of Zuni, in harshly beautiful painted desert country.

One branch of the ancestors of the Pueblo Indians - the Anasazis - settled in the Four Corners area of the southwest around the time of Christ. The other branch - the Mogollon culture - settled in southern New Mexico not long after. At first they were semi-nomadic tribes, growing crops when and where they could, living in pit houses, employing tightly woven baskets for food storage, transport and even cooking. As time went on they learned how to make pottery, constructed more elaborate and more permanent villages, and made advances in the fields of agriculture, religion, government and craftmaking.

But the southwestern deserts were - and are - a harsh place. Having enough water was a continuing problem. Raids from marauding Indian tribes never ceased. The great Pueblo Indian settlements at Mesa Verde, Chaco Canyon, Aztec and others were finally abandoned, the residents scattering in search of more security and better crop growing. In 1539 the first Europeans arrived, and the Pueblo tribes were faced with yet another threat to their traditional way of life : that of a powerful alien culture. The Puebloans accepted the Spaniards at first, but then began to resent their presence. All too often the Spanish military and church officials forced the Indians into servitude, took their stores of food, and gave them little choice about whether they should abandon traditional ways. In the end, rebellion was the violent reaction to the Spaniards' oppressive ways. In 1680 came the Pueblo Revolt, which drove the Spaniards completely from Pueblo lands.

But the Europeans were gone for only about a dozen years before they returned - this time to stay. The Puebloans had again to accomodate to the ways of a foreign culture. Again they had to find a way to survive.... The accomodating continues.

How long will the last remaining Pueblo cultures continue to retain their traditional identity in the face of such powerful influences for change? Only time will tell. The certainty is that the disappearance of these cultures, which thrived in North America long before the arrival of the first European explorers, would be a significant loss. It would mean the erasing of a vital link to the North American past.

If a traveler were to start at the northernmost pueblo of Taos and then proceeded to visit every pueblo in turn until reaching the westernmost villages of the Hopi, he would travel a total of perhaps 650 miles. A single, though hurried day's travel might do it. But a single day is far less than one should take if he would discover the Pueblo World. In a sense all of the pueblos are much the same - in the body type of the people, in basic lifestyle, in a world view, and in basic village architecture. But in other ways they are all truly different. Variations in

*In The Beginning*

physical environments, in language, in arts and crafts specialties, in cultural details and mythologies, differentiate one from the other. It would take much more than a single day to plumb the depths of the Pueblo Indian soul, his environment, and his approach to life. The Indians themselves refuse to be in such a great hurry. Neither should the visitor to their unique world.

*Touring The Pueblos*

## ABOUT YOUR VISIT

The sense of history and connection with an ancient past you receive are good enough reasons for a visit to the pueblo villages of the southwest. But there are other reasons too.

Pueblo Indian ceremonials are fascinating in and of themselves. The mesmerizing beat of drums, the chant of singers, the intricate weaving of the dancers, and the eye dazzling costumes give an air of primitive pageantry that is unforgettable. A bonus of a visit to a ceremonial is the authentic Indian food which is usually served, not to mention the rich display of arts and crafts to admire and perhaps buy.

There is pueblo architecture to admire. Most pueblos have dwellings that are both picturesque and historical. From the prehistoric period there is the Puye Cliff Dwelling complex located on the Santa Clara reservation, with its honeycomb of rock and mortar rooms. Almost as old are the mesa top villages of the Hopis and of Acoma, and the

## Touring The Pueblos

marvelous multi-storied "apartment houses" of the Taos Pueblo. More modern still, but still very old by any definition, are the early Spanish Colonial churches built under the direction of the Franciscans starting in the early 1600's. If only those thick adobe church walls - and the bell towers they support - could talk! What a story they could tell of religious dedication, of laborious effort, of privations, dangers, and of church excesses too.

The scenic setting of many of the pueblos is another good reason for taking the Pueblo Tour. Surrounding the Hopi lands are vast stretches of painted desert with pastel striations of magenta, cobalt blue, and emerald green shimmering through vast high desert space. In Zuni and Acoma territory are great flat topped mesas rising steeply from the desert floor like mystical, mythical tablets of stone. Surrounding the Jemez and Zia Pueblos are tablelands and cliffs which alternate between crimson, beige and orange. Rising to the east and west of the Eight Northern Pueblos of New Mexico are the Sangre de Cristo (Blood of Christ) Mountains, and the mountains of the Jemez, many peaks rising above 12,000 feet. Streams, lakes, rugged cliffs, Canadian forests, elk, deer, cougar, fox, coyote, all characterize these lands, which have changed little since the first mountain men and trappers arrived.

There are the Pueblo people themselves to contemplate and learn from. A wiry, thoughtful, deliberate, innovative, religious, independent, stoical, enduring and often very private people are the Pueblo Indians. Reservation lands constitute their mother, a refuge in times of 20th century stress; a bedrock of security which they can always return to if things get rough. Through

## About Your Visit

countless generations the Puebloans have learned something of the essence of life; learned what is important and what is not; resisted the impulse to become preoccupied with the frivolous concerns which mainstream Americans all too often get caught up in.

The pueblo visitor can also indulge in delights such as fishing, camping and picnicing. (See Appendix for listings.) Many pueblo lakes are stocked regularly with trout and other species. Several pueblos have campgrounds tailored specifically to accomodate travelers in RV's. Full hookups, showers, and convenience stores are offered by a few.

Finally, delightfully, there are Pueblo Indian arts and crafts to shop for and admire. The Indians and their ancestors - the Anasazi and Mogollon people - have been making pottery for more than 1,000 years. Potterymaking started out as a utilitarian craft dedicated to storing and cooking food. But after the settling of the American West, potterymaking became much more decorative and appealing to travelers. An eye-dazzling variety of shapes, sizes and colors was developed, most vessels made using the "old ways" of coiling and homemade firing. Pueblo jewelry-making began with objects made of wood, shells and stones, using crude tools. But then silver and turquoise came on the scene, along with more modern tools , and jewelry makers launched on a craftmaking journey that has elevated them to the level of world class artists. An amazing variety of silver pendants, rings, bracelets, necklaces, concho belts, and other forms, set with turquoise, coral, serpentine, shell and other colorful settings, are created by talented Indian artists.

But pottery and jewelry making aren't the only

## Touring The Pueblos

pueblo arts. There are storyteller figures, heishe necklaces, baskets, fetishes, weavings, mocassins, drums, alabaster sculptures, fine art paintings, and more, each pueblo with its own specialties. All pueblos have resident artists, some of them so well known as to be recognized all over the world for their talents.

However, any visitor to pueblo lands should remember that he or she is entering a private enclave - a country within a country - which has its own rules, regulations, law enforcement practices, traditions and taboos. Visitors are welcome at almost all the pueblos, but certain civilities and rules apply.

Keep an eye out for signs as you cross reservation boundaries - signs which explain what cautions and restrictions apply.

At ceremonials refrain from applauding, engaging in conversation with performers, photography or sketching, or any activity which might be disrespectful to what is, after all, a religious event.

Many pueblos have restrictions regarding photography, sketching and video production. When photography is allowed, often an established fee needs to be paid. When taking pictures of people, ask their permission first, with the offering of a monetary token of appreciation an established custom.

Alcoholic beverages and drugs are never allowed on pueblo lands.

Certain areas in a pueblo — kivas, cemeteries and private residences — are almost always off limits to outsiders.

Don't scramble on the walls of ages-old buildings and ruins. They have enough to worry about from the erosive effects of rain, snow, wind and frost, without

*About Your Visit*

the additional aging effects of physical abuse.

If these simple rules are observed, however, Pueblo people for the most part welcome visitors wholeheartedly to their traditional lands and homes.

Have a Happy Pueblo Tour!

*Touring The Pueblos*

# PART ONE

# EIGHT NORTHERN PUEBLOS

## Touring The Pueblos

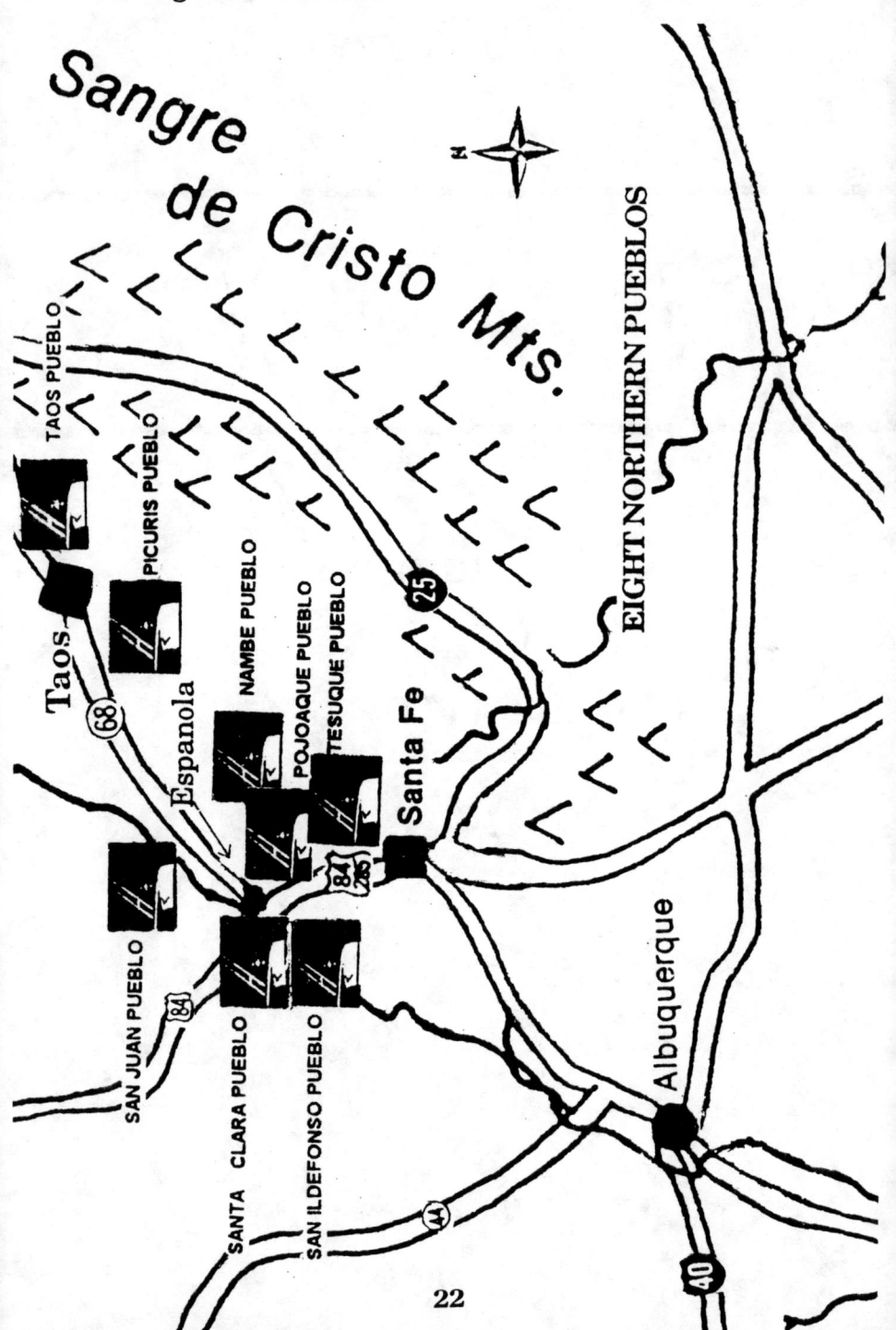

# TAOS

You reach this most-visited and northernmost of the pueblos by driving north on NM 68 from downtown Taos for about a mile until reaching the Taos Pueblo entrance road angling off to the right.

Highlights: *History and architecture.* The highest mountain peak in New Mexico rises behind the Tua-Tah ("Own Village")- or Taos - Pueblo, snow capping the crest of the towering Sangre de Cristo Mountains just to the east. In a depression on the near side of the high line of peaks lies sacred Blue Lake, out of which flows the cold, crystal clear waters of the Rio Pueblo de Taos, which nourishes the pueblo and its lands. Back in the old days a 20 foot high adobe wall surrounded this unique Indian village, where sentries would patrol as they kept a lookout for marauding Navajos, Comanches and Apaches. A massive gate stood at the entrance, always securely closed at nightfall after all the livestock was driven inside to safety. Right from its start back in the early 1400's, Taos' survival depended on diligent watchfulness and adherence to tight security measures.

## Touring The Pueblos

It was in the summer of 1680 when a wily, charismatic medicine man named Popay traveled north to Taos from his native San Juan pueblo on urgent business. After five years of thinking and planning the time had come to unite the Pueblo people in driving the Spanish interlopers from their homeland. The Puebloans had welcomed the newcomers when they first arrived 140 years before. But gradually the forced imposition of European customs and religion, the taxes, servitude and harsh punishments, brought deep resentment among the Indians. An early portent of the future occurred in 1639 when the Taos tribe revolted in a shortlived episode, burning the mission church and killing the local friar. By 1680 things had truly reached the flash point. Popay met with the chiefs and shamans of other pueblo tribes and slowly they developed a plan. This time there must be an all-encompassing uprising, and it must not fail. A date was finally settled upon for the revolt - August 11 - and knotted ropes were sent by courier to the other tribes to signal the exact date. But as the time grew near, priests at one pueblo learned of the plan, forcing Popay to advance the start of the rebellion by one day. Thus, 140 years after the first arrival of Spanish explorers, the great Pueblo Revolt began. Almost immediately 70 Spanish settlers in the Taos area were summarily killed by the Indians, with but two survivors. As the revolt gathered steam, the Spaniards fled to battlements behind the Governor's Palace in Santa Fe. Outside the enclave thousands of Pueblo Indian warriors gathered and mounted a siege which was to last for five hellish days. Finally, in an act of pure desperation, the Spanish soldiers gathered themselves and mounted a desperate counterattack on

*Taos*

the massed Indian warriors. The action killed hundreds, scattering the rest. In the confusion which followed, the besieged Spanish were able to leave their fortifications and flee southward, leaving most of their possessions behind. The Indians let them go. Thus had the Europeans been driven completely from pueblo lands for the first time since their arrival. The Puebloans proceeded to celebrate a great victory as they went about destroying all traces of the hated Spanish presence.

...But of course the Europeans weren't gone for very long. In only a dozen years they returned. After some initial skirmishes and intense diplomacy they regained a foothold in Pueblo country. A more harmonious relationship with the Indians developed over time, and Spanish settlements multiplied without further resistance from the Indians.

*Taos Pueblo "apartment house" complex*

But there was one more battle to come at the Taos Pueblo. In 1847, a year after the American Army of the West rode into Santa Fe and took possession of New Mexico Territory without firing a shot, there were grumblings by both the ousted Mexicans and the Taos Indians regarding the new order of things. Helped along with generous amounts of "Taos Lightning," members of the disgruntled faction undertook to scalp and kill Governor-General Charles Bent one night. It was a hostile act, which could not go unpunished. Thus did American Colonel Sterling Price ride north from Santa Fe with troops to settle the matter. The Taos Indians resisted the incursion and fought bravely, using the thick-walled mission church as their stronghold. Colonel Price started shelling the mission at nine in the morning, and it took until 3:30 that afternoon before the walls were breached. It was all over then. Some 250 Taos Indians finally lay dead from the battle, with more hanged later. It turned out to be the last campaign mounted against the Pueblo Indians, in a history full of military campaigns.

Today, the ruins of the old embattled mission rest much as they were left after that 1847 battle. The same bell hangs from a restored mission bell tower. An overgrown cemetery lies before the ruins, with other more recent dead laid beside the original fallen warriors.

But not much else was damaged in that furious battle so long ago. The architecture of the Taos Pueblo - its best known feature - remains much as it has been since the mid 1400's when it was built. This great "apartment house" of an Indian village - the largest of its kind still occupied - has been the subject of countless artistic renderings, photographic compositions, and travel illustrations over the years, drawing visitors from the world over. No wonder that the Taos Pueblo has been designated a National Historic Site, and been designated the 15th American Site in the World Heritage Convention - a world list which includes the Taj Mahal and the Great Pyramids.

There are two multi-storied, golden brown building complexes made of mud and straw, one on the north side of the Rio Pueblo de Taos (known originally as Willow Creek), and the other on the south side. To this day there is no electricity, indoor plumbing, or running water in the old pueblo. The more impressive of the two complexes is the one on the north, which stands five stories high and once housed within its thick adobe walls several hundred people. It is only since the turn of the century that doorways and windows have been built into the south facing walls to allow sunlight in and the easy entrance of its occupants. Before that, almost all of the rooms were entered via ladders from the top, to provide greater security. Many families still live in the old pueblo (the remainder of the tribe lives in more modern dwellings nearby), most often in two rooms, the front one used for living and sleeping, the rear for cooking, eating and storage. Small vent holes allow smoke from fireplaces (adapted from the Spanish) which, if the dwellings are to be occupied during the cold high desert winters, must be kept burning for weeks beforehand so the walls can absorb heat. There are no interconnecting passageways from one family unit to the other, so the occupant on one side of a connecting wall must go out and enter from the outside. The adobe walls are as much as two feet thick in places, the roofs made by laying timbers (*vigas*) across the

*Touring The Pueblos*

tops of the walls, with smaller branches between, filling in the spaces with mud plaster. You'll often see Taos men nowadays adding new mud plaster to walls and roofs to counteract the effects of erosion. In the large open space between the two building complexes are drying racks (little used today) traditionally employed to dry meat, fruits and produce. Near the entranceway of this historic place is the St. Jerome Church, impressive in design and dramatic in contrasting hues of brown and white, built after that famous battle of 1847. It rests on the site of the original church built by the Spanish in the 1600's. This Spanish Colonial style church adds a fascinating counterpoint to the more primitive roof lines of one of the most compelling primitive dwelling complexes seen anywhere.

The Taos Pueblo is open to visitors every day

*Taos Pottery*

starting at 8 AM. You'll pay a modest entrance fee (and another fee if you wish to take pictures, sketch or paint), but the guided tours are offered free of charge (though gratuities are accepted). You're welcome to wander any areas which don't have "off limit" signs (which includes the ceremonial kivas and private residences).

   Shopping - Many of the ground level rooms have been converted to shop spaces, and that's where you'll find some unique shopping opportunities. Doeskin mocassins are a Taos Indian specialty. Indian blankets are yet another. The Taos Pueblo is also one of the few to continue making micaceous pottery - the hard fired type which can be used for cooking. Other items include Taos-made concho belts, storyteller figures, handmade drums, and many types of jewelry.

   Eating - The smell of cedar and pinon smoke is usually in the air from domed *hornos* (beehive) ovens and grills, telling of baking bread and Indian frybread for sale under thatched ramadas. Try *Maria Concha's* and *Crucita's Indian Shop* for fresh baked bread and other Indian cuisine.

   Recreation - An outfit called the *Taos Indian Horse Ranch* (P.O. Box 3019, Taos, NM 87571, Ph. (505) 758-3212) offers a variety of horse riding activities, cook-outs, pack trips, photo safaris and Indian dances on Taos lands.

   Ceremonials - There are number of ceremonials which this Tiwa speaking tribe holds each year, most of which are open to the public. They include the San Geronimo Feast Day on September 30, and the Taos Pow Wow in July. The pow wow commemorates the old days when Taos was well known as a trading center, catering to the needs of other Indian tribes (including their

## Touring The Pueblos

traditional enemies operating under truce conditions), as well as Mexicans from Chihuahua, European trappers, traders and mountain men, and also new American settlers. Today's visitor will find much the same in shopping opportunities, entertainment and merriment, though in more modern guise.

For more information regarding this much visited and northernmost of the pueblos, contact: Taos Pueblo Tourism, P.O. Box 1846, Taos, NM 87571 Ph. (505) 758-8626, or 758-9593.

St. Jerome Mission Church at Taos Pueblo

## PICURIS

The most used route to the Picuris (pronounced Pee-kur-ee) Pueblo is via NM 68 to the intersection with NM 75 (20 miles south of Taos), then east on NM 75. You'll climb gradually to the top of a ridge of the Sangre de Cristo foothills, then drop down into Hidden Valley, the home of the Picuris people.

Highlight: *micaceous pottery*.

The tribe, with a population of about 270, is small now, but it hasn't always been so. At one point back around 1600, Picuris was one of the two largest pueblos (along with now extinct Pecos Pueblo). In 1621 Fray Martin de Arvide ministered to some 2,000 Picuris Indians out of a population of around 3,000. But relentless attacks by marauding tribes, the ravages of European diseases, and an outright temporary abandonment of the village at one point, led to a steep decline in population. The isolation of the tribe in a remote valley has encouraged self reliance, hardiness, and the quality of endurance. Thus the pueblo survives, and slowly gains in population. Indians have lived in this area since about 900 AD, but the Picuris tribe

## Touring The Pueblos

didn't come here to Hidden Valley until about 1250, after abandoning previous settlements in the Pot Creek area, further north. The tribe is most closely related to the Taos Indians. It was warriors from both the Taos and Picuris tribes which bore the brunt of the fighting during the Pueblo Revolt of 1680. A measure of the Picuris prowess as warriors is seen in the fact that one of the top leaders during the Revolt - Luis Tapatu - led the attacks on the Spanish garrison at Santa Fe.

A most noteworthy aspect of the Picuris Pueblo is its continuing expertise at making ages-old, highly utilitarian *micaceous pottery*. The flashing silver and gold specks of mica in the clay found in these northern mountains helps to produce a hardened, watertight, heat treated ceramic very suitable for cooking use - something you can't generally say about the more widely produced decorative potteryware. Whether pueblo pottery is of the micaceous or decorative type, however, what sets it apart from commercial ware is the use of *traditional methods* in its fabrication. This is a primary reason why Indian-made pottery has become so much in demand by collectors and buyers in general.

Following, in a nutshell, is the *traditional* method of pueblo potterymaking.

The first step is to gather the clay. The pueblo potter tends to be very secretive about where her (or his, in some cases) mother lode of specialized clay is located. In the case of the Picuris potter, shovels-full of mica bearing material are put into buckets of water, where the debris can be separated out and the clay softened. The clay is then allowed to dry to a stiff-but-moist state, for easy working. If the clay is too pure, a tempering material

## Picuris

- sand, ground potsherds, crushed rock - may be added to prevent excessive stickiness or the possibility of cracking during firing. (The mica in micaceous clay usually makes additional temper unnecessary.) The clay is then kneaded to remove air bubbles and to yield uniform moistness. The clay is ready to be formed into the desired shape then. A flat base is formed and installed on a tray or bowl-like fixture called a *puki.*, to provide support and allow easier turning. Coils of clay are added successfully, one on top of the other and pinched together, until the wall of the vessel is complete. The wavy top is trimmed off flat and the sides scraped smooth using a wooden paddle, pottery piece, or other smoothing tool. The pot is then allowed to dry for awhile before pieces of sandstone or other sanding mediums are employed to smooth the inside and outside surfaces. Mica bearing clay is inherently stronger than most other types, making thinner walls possible. The next step involves the application of slip - a creamy mixture of fine, wet clay - to add characteristic color, to seal the rough surface, and to present a more polished appearance. An ultra smooth stone is finally used to polish the surface to a fine finish after drying. For firing the pot is place upside down on a supporting surface made of stones or metalwork. A wood fire is built underneath to warm the earth, then a hotter fire - using sticks, bark or dung - serves to give a hard firing to the pots. The result in the micaceous pot is a bronze-gold color, often with a characteristic fire cloud pattern appearing where pieces of wood or fuel have leaned against the pot during firing. A wide variety of shapes are possible, ranging from fat bean pots with handles (it's been said that beans never taste better than when cooked in a micaceous pot), to storage jugs, to sugar

## Touring The Pueblos

bowls and tea pots, to a variety of other shapes. In the case of micaceous pots, decoration is limited to minor incisions and applique. The beautiful, practical micaceous form of pottery has been around since at leaast the early 1600's, with a rougher version in use long before that. Smaller, rougher micaceous pots can be bought for much less than $100, with the finest selling for $2,000 or more. Nowadays, the making of micaceous ware has spread to other pueblos besides Picuris and Taos, which have long been noted for this specialty.

    A tour of the Picuris Pueblo should begin at the *Picuris Pueblo Museum*, where you can pay the modest visting fee, and be given a tourguide/map. If you want to take pictures, a photo fee is charged. The ruins of the original church, built in the 1620's, is located just across the road from the museum/restaurant/general store, next to the *Picuris Pueblo Enterprise*, which offers a variety of Indian wares for sale. At the top of the hill to the north is the site of the original pueblo, with several fascinating ruins. One of them is an above-ground "tower" kiva (ceremonial chamber), built more than 400 years ago, and the only one of its type still surviving. *Castillo Viejo* (Old Castle) is the name given to the section of rooms next to the "tower," now in ruins except for low walls of adobe. There was a time, long ago, when these walls rose to six or more stories, housing many families. In fields on both sides of the Rio Pueblo at the base of the hill, ancestors of these Indians would raise squash, beans, corn and other crops, even though the growing season is short here. Today Picuris residents continue to grow these and other crops and engage in a number artistic endeavors. Scattered among more modern dwellings you will see a number of old stone and adobe homes, giving a sense of how this village looked centuries ago. It is the village elders who tend to live in these more traditional abodes now.

   <u>Shopping</u> - Micaceous pottery, weaving, paintings and jewelry items are for sale at the *Picuris Pueblo Enterprise* across from the museum, and at the museum itself. Arts and crafts can also be bought at the homes of artists who have crafts signs displayed out front. Indian-made wares are also offered at the *High Country Tri-Cultural Arts and Crafts Fair*, which takes place the first week in July, and at all ceremonials open to the public. In addition, the Picuris Pueblo owns the only tribally owned arts and crafts store in Santa Fe, in the gift shop of the majority owned Hotel Santa Fe - a fine hotel built in the Pueblo Revival style.

   <u>Eating</u> - Both Indian and American food are available at the *Hidden Valley Restaurant* next to the museum, open 7 days a week during the summer, 11 AM to 7 PM. Breakfast 9 AM to Noon on Sundays only. Winter hours are 11:30 AM to 6 PM Monday, Wednesday and Thursday; 11:30 AM to 7 PM Fri-Sun. Closed Tuesdays.

   <u>Recreation</u> - Guided tours of the Picuris Pueblo are available (check at the museum). Take a tour of the museum itself for a good overview of Picuris history, and of its historical artifacts. You can fish for trout and catfish at the two tribal lakes, *Pu-Na* and *Tu-Tah*. Fees are $4 for both adults and children.

   <u>Ceremonials</u> - Annual events open to the public are those on Easter Sunday, on June 13, July 5 and 6, and those held during the annual feast days of August 9-10, which feature a sunset dance the first evening, and a Clown Society pole climb, races and dances the following

*Touring The Pueblos*

day. As at most pueblos, other unscheduled ceremonials are held at short notice throughout the year. For dates and times, check with tribal offices.

For further information contact: Picuris Enterprises, Pueblo of Picuris, P.O. Box 487, Penasco NM 87553. Ph. (505) 587-2957.

*Old wagon at Picuris Pueblo.*

# SAN JUAN

San Juan Pueblo is located about 5 miles north of Espanola, New Mexico, just west of NM 68. Watch for a sign.

Highlights: *Political leadership*; annual *Eight Northern Indian Pueblo Artists and Craftsman Show* often held here.

This cottonwood-shaded pueblo — largest of the Tewa pueblos, with a population of about 1800 - was established about 700 years ago. In 1598, 22 years before the Pilgrims founded the Plymouth colony, Spanish conquistador Juan de Onate arrived here with 400 soldiers and was so impressed by the friendliness of the San Juan people (the village was called *Ok'e* - "We are the brothers" - then) that he made it the capitol of *Nuevo Mexico* and changed the name to *San Gabriel*. It remained the capitol until a more permanent one was established at Santa Fe, 10 years later. San Juan was the birthplace and home of the pueblo world's most famous leader - Popay - who led the great Pueblo Revolt of 1680. As it turned out, the San Juan people were a bit too patient with the oppressive

## Touring The Pueblos

ways of the Spanish to suit Popay, so he moved the base of his rebellion further north to Taos. But come the time for the uprising, all the San Juans joined in the battle to oust the Spaniards.

Unlike some of the pueblos, there are no fascinating ruins to be seen here, no ancient multi-story dwellings, no breathtaking mesa-top vistas, or even historical battles. On the other hand, San Juan did, and still does have a talent for tribal administration. As mentioned, it was the original capitol of *Nuevo Mexico*. And now it's the seat of the Eight Northern Indian Pueblos Council - an administrative body founded for the purpose of advancing social service needs of the pueblos, and in promoting tourism and the marketing of pueblo arts and crafts. San

*New England style church at San Juan Pueblo.*

*San Juan*

Juan is also the headquarters of the Northern Pueblos Agency of the Bureau of Indian Affairs. The Pueblo North Market Center is part of the Eight Northern Indian Pueblos Council, and through it vocational training in the arts and crafts is conducted, and new markets developed worldwide.

San Juan is located within a heavily cottonwooded section of the Rio Grande *bosque*, and the groves of trees (especially during the leafed-out months of April to November) is a distinguishing and beautiful characteristic which sets this pueblo apart from all others. As you go on a walking tour (no fee for exploring, but you'll need to pay a fee at the Governor's office for still, movie or video photography, and for sketching) you'll find only about 100 of the 700 year old adobe buildings remaining, and no sign of the former San Gabriel presence. Even the original Spanish church tumbled into ruins in 1913, and was never rebuilt. But a New England style church and chapel (The Lady of Lourdes, built in 1889) stand out across from each other on the main thoroughfare, striking as much by their contrast with other buildings as anything else.

If any of San Juan's handicrafts stand it out it is probably pottery - an art form which is of the earth, and which serves to define the essence of the pueblo world itself. In the old days San Juan pottery was an undecorated ware, of polished red over beige, or black over gray. A more modern trademark feature is the addition of incised lines arranged in geometric patterns for decoration. This distinctive style was taken from the old *Potsui 'i* style of the late 15th century, found in ancient sherds from ancestral ruins.

*Touring The Pueblos*

<u>Shopping</u> - The products of San Juan artists are presented most notably through the *O'ke Oweenge Arts and Crafts Cooperative,* established in 1968. It's located just east of the churches noted above, and is where you'll find examples from most all the Indian crafts. In the cool **interior of the Pueblo Style complex are silver/turquoise** jewelry items, pottery, alabaster sculptures, cast bronzes, wood carvings, mocassins, weavings, and fine arts - not only by San Juan artists, but by those of other pueblos as well. A bonus of a visit to *Aguino's Indian Arts and Crafts Shop* (located just east of the pueblo center) is that of witnessing arts and crafts workshops in progress (check with Juan Aguino re: scheduling, at P.O. Box 52, San Juan Pueblo, NM 87566; or Ph. (505) 753-9168). A true extravaganza of arts and crafts shopping can be enjoyed by visiting the annual *Eight Northern Indian Pueblos Artist and Craftsman Show*, often held at the San Juan Pueblo in July (call the San Juan Governor's Office for exact location and dates). It's one of the major such events in the pueblo world, with hundreds of booths and 800 to 1,000 Indian craftsmen exhibiting from all over the American west and beyond. In addition to arts and crafts of course, there is always food at this prestigious event - Indian, Mexican and American - plus dances and other doings. More information available by writing: ENIPC, Inc., P.O. Box 969, San Juan Pueblo, NM 87566. Ph. (505) 852-4265.

<u>Eating</u> - The *Tewa Indian Restaurant* (located on the main thoroughfare, near the center of the pueblo) features Indian frybread, blue corn maiden, red and green chile stew, posole, and Indian teas, to name a few menu items. The restaurant is open 9 AM to 2:30 PM Monday

## San Juan

through Friday.

<u>Recreation</u> - Fishing and picnicing can be enjoyed at *San Juan Tribal Lakes and Recreation*, located within the city limits of nearby Espanola. Shelters and picnic tables are situated around the lakes, but no overnight camping. Fees are: $7 for adults for 4 catches per day; $4 for children for 4 catches per day. Seniors pay $4 for 8 catches per day. Hours are sunrise to sunset during the summer, and 8 AM to 5 PM in winter.

*San Juan Pueblo Bingo* is offered Wednesday through Sunday evenings, with doors opening at 5:30 and games starting at 7 PM. Sunday afternoons the doors open at noon and games begin at 1 PM. The bingo parlor is located 3 miles north of Espanola on NM 68.

*Ceremonials* - The annual San Juan Feast Day is June 24, but other events are scheduled on short notice throughout the year.

For further information contact: Governor's Office, P.O. Box 1099, San Juan Pueblo, NM 87566. Ph. (505) 852-4400.

*Touring The Pueblos*

## SANTA CLARA

You'll find Santa Clara Pueblo about a mile and a half south of Espanola, New Mexico, on NM 30.

Highlights: *Puye Cliff Dwellings; red and black pottery.*

The Puye Cliff Dwellings are owned and operated by the Santa Clara tribe itself, and you reach them by driving 4 miles southwest of Espanola on NM 30 to the entrance of Santa Clara Canyon. You'll proceed 7 miles up a paved access road to the cliffs. Santa Clara is fortunate to have a complete prehistoric village ruin of its Anasazi forbears. You'll see the two levels of cliff ruins as you approach the cliffs, almost invisible at first, but then discernable in the form of disintegrating walls and enlarged recesses in the tufa cliffs, extending for a mile or more along the cliff face. Some dwellings built into the cliff sides once soared to three stories. The Puebloans took up residence here in about 1450 AD, but abandoned the complex in about 1550 due to lack of water. They moved to their present fertile valley location, near the ever flowing Rio Grande. During the Pueblo Revolt they once

*Touring The Pueblos*

again returned to their ancient homestead to wait out the expected retribution by the Spaniards. But they soon returned.

It's not hard to imagine the way it was here at Puye 700 years ago, as fields were worked on top of the mesa and below, water transported in large clay *ollas*, the food and water balanced precariously on heads and strong backs as crude ladders were negotiated to reach cliffside apartments. Many rooms were closed in by masonry walls for protection from sometimes fierce winter weather. Children had to be watched carefully of course, and taught from an early age how to avoid falling from the edge of vertical cliffs. Today, trails lead to the base of the

*Puye Cliff Dwelling complex*

## Santa Clara

cliff, and part way up, where ladders extend almost to the top of the mesa where an even more fascinating vista awaits. (There's also an improved road to the top, for visitors not wanting to climb the "old way" via pinon pole ladders.) From here you overlook the verdant Santa Clara Canyon and Espanola Valley, with the soaring Sangre de Cristos further east. Spread out across the mesa top is a ruined village of impressive proportions. A vast honeycomb of stone-walled rooms sits basking under the shimmering New Mexico sun. There were some 750 rooms at the time of peak occupation, housing some 1500 Puye people. A square kiva stands at the northern edge (accessible to visitors), a large community house at the opposite end. Both the cliff side and cliff top dwellings were occupied at the same time. The Anasazis ("The Ancient Ones") took up residence at Puye after leaving the Four Corners region. These fascinating ruins are open 8 AM to 6 PM every day in summer, 8 AM to 4 PM in winter. A modest fee ($4 for adults, $3 for children 7-14, $3 for seniors) is payable at the entrance.

An additional Santa Clara highlight is highly prized, highly polished red and black pottery. The pueblo has been a center of distinctive pottery for centuries, the vessels often decorated with a distinctive "bear claw" impression. The carved "water serpent" impression (reminding you of water channels in a flood plain) is another trademark feature. Water storage bowls, double spouted, strap handled wedding jars, melon bowls, seed jars, and many other pottery forms take shape at the hands of skilled Santa Clara potters. The distinctive black color of some of the pieces is achieved during the firing process, where oxidizing and temperature are controlled precisely, along with specialized selection of fuel for the fire. The result is a deep, striking black, which is carefully, painstakingly polished using natural stones and other materials. But before firing and polishing, an additional hallmark feature of Santa Clara pottery is often added: after the vessel has been formed using traditional methods, a relief carving step takes place, where the somewhat dry, thick walled pot receives the bite of various carving tools, the background cut away to leave a bold, raised relief patterns of water serpent forms, animal figures, flower forms, mythic symbols, and other designs. The individual elements are often delicate and fragile enough to break off during carving and polishing, ruining hours of work. Experimentation has long been part of the Santa Clara potterymaking tradition, with potters constantly on the lookout for new clays, new varieties of slip to give new colors and effects, and new ways of firing.

The pueblo village isn't quite as picturesque as the Puye ruins and Santa Clara Canyon areas, but well worth a visit - especially if you want to shop for the splendid handmade pottery and other wares offered by local artists. The Tewa word for the Santa Clara people is *Khapo*, meaning "Singing Water," and it's somewhat apropos considering the upbeat friendliness of the residents here. You'll drive by the administrative center on the west side of the main thoroughfare not far from the entrance, and that's where you need to pay a still camera fee of $4 ($10 for movie and video cameras, and $15 for sketching), if you have these activities in mind. No fee for general exploration of the pueblo however. One edifice worth photographing or sketching is the mission church, just down the road from the admin center. It's unusual in its striking

*Santa Clara*

narrowness, and the charming off-center bell tower. Just south of the mission is a small plaza with several shops, some with gaily painted borders around their windows, in the Spanish style.

<u>Shopping</u> - There are a goodly number of shops selling Indian wares in this pueblo, some located around the small plaza noted above, others within the private dwellings of artists. Pottery isn't the only item Santa Clara artists create of course. Fine paintings, sculptures, embroidery, wood carvings, beadwork and jewelry are also created here. The *Butterfly Balloon Shop* is one of the shops, offering a full line of craft items, and also educational tours of the pueblo and its lands. (Call (505) 753-5657 for further information.) *Singing Water Pottery and Tours* is another well known gallery, located on Highway 30 near the pueblo entrance. This shop too offers a full range of Native American crafts and tours of the local area. (Call (505) 753-9663). Other well known shops include the *Toni Roller Pottery and Green Leaves Studio*, the *Corn Studio*, the *Merrock Galerie*, and the *Native Arts Studio*. Crafts are also offered at the annual public festival at the Puye Cliff Dwellings. (Check with the Governor's Office for details.)

<u>Recreation</u> - Santa Clara has a star attraction in its *Santa Clara Canyon* area, located beyond the cliff dwellings. Four lakes and a stream offer fishing (adults $10 for 8 catches of trout/catfish per day, children $5 for 4 catches). The canyon is open sunrise to sunset every day from April to October. Picnicing, sightseeing and hiking on the trails which wind through pine, spruce and aspen forests available for $8 per vehicle per day. In addition, Santa Clara offers camping at 86 campsites, with one

sheltered cabin available. Water and toilet facilities available. The on-duty tribal ranger will answer questions and collect the $10 per night camping fee. The pueblo itself offers its own tours too, which can include native dancing, arts and craftmaking demo's, and Indian food. A recent addition to Santa Clara's reportoire is river running on the Rio Grande. Call five days ahead re: resevations for these tours.

<u>Ceremonials</u> - The annual feast day is August 12, but there are unscheduled events throughout the year.

For additional information contact: Tourism Department, Pueblo of Santa Clara, P.O. Box 580, Espanola NM 87532. Ph. (505) 753-7326.

# SAN ILDEFONSO

From Santa Fe you reach San Ildefonso Pueblo by driving 16 miles north on NM 84 to the intersection with NM 502, then west 6 miles to the San Ildefonso turnoff.

Highlight: *Black on black pottery.*

A 200-plus year old cottonwood tree is a striking feature of the San Ildefonso (*Powohgeoweenge*, in the Tewa language - meaning "where the water cuts through") Pueblo, and one wonders what life was like here at the time the big tree was but a sapling. The mesas on both sides of the valley were still heavily forested back then, compared to their more denuded condition now. The population was bustling, not yet victim of the smallpox epidemic which struck in 1918, reducing tribal numbers to less than 100. (Population is about 500 now.) By that time, 200-plus years ago, it had been almost a century since the tribe fled to nearby Tunyon Mesa to escape the expected Spanish onslaught after the Reconquest of 1592. They stayed there until just about every other pueblo had made their peace with the Spaniards. Finally they did return though, to resume growing crops of beans and corn in nearby fields, storing the harvest in pots covered with rawhide... And meanwhile the cottonwood continued to grow and grow, witnessing an untold number of tribal dances and games and religious ceremonies in the main plaza. The cottonwood also witnessed a dispute after the 1918 smallpox epidemic which led to a split of the pueblo into two plazas as part of an attempt to change the run of the pueblo's bad luck. Much has changed in the 200-plus year life of the cottonwood all right, in this modest size village beside the Rio Grande.

A Visitor Center is situated at the south entrance, where you can pick up a map/tourguide. The daily admission fee is $3, with a still camera permit costing $5, a movie/video fee $15. The map/tourguide will direct you to the *San Ildefonso Pueblo Museum*, among other places, located next to the mission church and in the complex which houses the offices of the Governor. The museum features a diorama showing the traditional pueblo method of potterymaking and, significantly, a collection of the trademark San Ildefonso pottery style: black-on-black. It's the style which made this pueblo famous, and which is largely credited with rekindling the potterymaking spirit throughout the pueblo world. If any of the pueblos can be said to be famous for certain of its artists, it is this one. For this was the home of Julian and Maria Martinez, who reached the level of "star" status for the black-on-black style which they revived and made famous. It was in 1918 when archaeologists working at the Tsankawi ruins in nearby Bandelier National Monument (one of the pueblo's ancestral homes) came across sherds of an impressive style of prehistoric pottery. Maria Martinez, already an experienced potter, was asked to try and

## San Ildefonso

duplicate the style, and she set about the task. It didn't take her long to produce high quality, thin walled pots like those at Tsankawi, which husband Julian proceeded to decorate with fine black lines. The pair began to experiment with an oxidizing process then, which cut short the firing via the smothering of the fire with manure. The result was a striking jet black finish. The vessels were polished to a mirror-like sheen using smooth streambed stones, and the result was magnificent indeed. A further variation - one which truly set the Martinez style apart from all others - came about when Julian used Maria's clay slip to paint his own unique designs. The result - after firing - was to produce a matte black finish side by side with the

*San Ildefonso Pueblo Plaza*

## Touring The Pueblos

shiny black, which was (and is) highly distinctive. Buyers responded by purchasing all the Martinez pots they could get their hands on. Critics praised them, museums collected them, and thus was a potterymaking legend born. There was a snowball effect, as the popularity of the Martinez style led to a general resurgence of interest in handmade pueblo pottery. Soon, potterymaking ceased to be only for ceremonial and utilitarian uses. Potterymaking became a commercially viable profession for pueblo artists, with aesthetics becoming as important as symbology as keys in decoration. Today, San Ildefonso continues the black-on-black tradition, as most families - including the heirs of the Martinezes - continue in potterymaking. Early on, Maria Martinez was happy to get 50 cents for one of her creations. Nowadays, $75,000 isn't uncommon for one of her large jars. The plumed water serpent and Mimbres feather designs (began by the Mimbres people of southern New Mexico in the 9th-11th centuries) are still seen on many of the vessels. Black-on-black isn't the only style seen here of course. Noted potter Blue Corn (who became the pueblo's "star" after Maria and Julian died) has always been inclined toward polychrome ware. Others do red and black ware, relief carved designs with inlaid turquoise, and sgrafito. Maria Martinez' original work can be seen at the *Popovi Da Studio of Indian Arts* at San Ildefonso, on request, in a special private museum.

    A tour of San Ildefonso takes you past pueblo style homes with protruding *vigas* and columned porches, a few obviously very old, most of more modern vintage. The church is a reconstruction of that original Spanish mission built in 1617, which fell into ruins and was rebuilt in 1711. That church, too, was destroyed, to be rebuilt in 1904. One

## San Ildefonso

more rebuilding was to take place on the site before the current reconstruction was complete in 1968. Near the church stands the so called "Hollywood Gate," of heavy, aging timbers, built in the 1940's as a prop for a couple of western movies made here. The raising of crops has always been a San Ildefonso mainstay, and continues to be, in the flat, fertile fields by the side of the Rio Grande. Off to the west rise the red-beige foothills of the Jemez Mountains, with blue-tinged high country rising steeply beyond. To the northeast rises Black Mesa, where in 1694 the tribe held off 100 well armed Spanish troops led by de Vargas. The siege lasted five days, but Spanish victory was pretty much a forgone conclusion. The Spanish had learned something from the Pueblo Revolt of 1680, however. After the Reconquest they made more of an effort to accomodate the Puebloans and their way of life. It helped. For the most part, Spanish/Indian problems were resolved peaceably in the ensuing years. To the east of the pueblo rise the magnificent Sangre de Cristos, snow often remaining on north facing slopes throughout the summer.

   Shopping - Pottery, ribbon shirts, embroidery and other Indian wares are for sale at the Visitor and Information Center at the south entrance. (Hours: 8 AM to 5 PM every day during the summer, closed on weekends in winter.) The aforementioned *Popovi Da Studio of Indian Arts* has pottery, jewelry, paintings and other items for sale. The *Aguilar Indian Arts Shop* specializes in red and black pottery, but has a full range of other Indian wares too. *Juan Tafoya Pottery* specializes in traditional black-on-black pottery and red siena pottery. *Torres Indian Arts* has black-on-black too, plus other styles and other wares.

Generally the shops are open from 10 AM to 5 PM on weekdays.

<u>Ceremonials</u> - January 6 is Reyes Day; January 22 is when evening fireflight dances take place. January 23 is the annual feast day. Various dances also take place on Easter Sunday, with Corn Dances in June, late August and early September. There are always activities at Christmas time, too, including the famous Matachina Dances. Check with tribal offices for exact dates and times.

For further information contact: Governor's Office, Pueblo of San Ildefonso, Route 5, Box 315-A, Santa Fe NM 87501 Ph. (505) 455-2273.

# NAMBE

You reach Nambe ("Mound of earth in the corner") Pueblo from Santa Fe by driving northeast on U.S. 84 for 15 miles until reaching the junction with NM 503, where you'll turn right and proceed for 3 1/2 miles to the Nambe Pueblo access road and another right turn.

Highlight: *Nambe Falls Recreation Area.*

This small (population: 600) pueblo was established about 700 years ago. Not much of the original village remains now, except for the round kiva and a couple of dozen precolonial dwellings. The original picturesque mission church tumbled into ruins in 1909, to be replaced by a more modern version. If you're at the pueblo during a ceremonial, you'll experience a true sense of time warp upon seeing Elk Dancers going through ritual steps atop the age-old kiva, summoning the benevolence of sacred spirits.

As you drive toward the entrance to the old village you'll see sculptural sandstone spires rising off to the left, and straight ahead the majestic Sangre de Cristos going

## Touring The Pueblos

up and up. A right turn leads you down a dirt road to the old pueblo. No fee for casual sightseeing, but a still camera fee of $3 is charged if you want to take pictures. The fee for movie/video cameras is $5, and $10 for sketching. You can pay fees and ask questions at the tribal administrative building on the right as you enter the pueblo grounds.

The standout feature of Nambe is *Nambe Falls*, located in the foothills behind the pueblo. Nambe Creek rises between Baldy and Lake Peaks high in the Sangre de Cristos, flowing through steep canyons and heavily forested tablelands until reaching Nambe Lake, and below it an abrupt cliff where it throws itself into empty space for breathtaking white water moments before crashing into smooth rocks below. It is the only modern pueblo with such a watery wonder. (Some of the pueblo ancestors had *Frijoles Falls*, now part of Bandelier National Monument, to enjoy and marvel at.)

Nambe Falls is representative of the majestic, timeless quality of the natural environment which surrounds much of the Pueblo World. The falls, fed by snow pack and underground aquifers, was sending its flashing white tendrils through space when the Nambe Indians first arrived in the 1300's. It continued, undiminished, several hundred years later when the Europeans arrived and felt of its cool spray. (The falls varied in volumne more back then, before the dam below the lake was built.) The falls kept on plummeting downward during the Pueblo Revolt and the Reconquest which followed. Mountain men came and trapped for beaver pelts in this and countless other streams and lakes on these southern flanks of the Rocky Mountains. Plains Indians would continue as they had for centuries to make

*Nambe*

*Nambe Falls*

their way west through stately pine forests above Nambe, enroute to a raid on the Rio Grande pueblos perhaps, or a bit of trading, or maybe both. Miners too came to the Sangre de Cristos and Jemez Mountains, staking claims, setting up towns, then abandoning them when the precious metal ran out. In the surrounding area the owners of Spanish land grants and their wards settled in to scratch out a hard living on stubborn soil, building their homes always with an eye to protection from marauding Apaches, Navajos and Comanches. The year 1846 came then, and the Americans took over New Mexico Territory from the Mexicans without firing a shot. Statehood for New Mexico followed, and meanwhile there was a continuation of the decaying process in the dwellings of the old Nambe Indian village. More roads were built here in the northern Rio Grande Valley. More people came... And meanwhile Nambe Falls kept right on thundering, arching downward through slanting space, unstoppable. It's no wonder that Pueblo Indians set so much store by Mother Earth. For you can count on Mother Earth. The rules which she establishes don't change. No wonder that the Nambes - and other pueblo tribes - were often such a tough sell to the early missionaries, who all too often failed to stick to the ideals they preached.

<u>Shopping</u> - On July 4 Nambe Falls sees the annual *Nambe Waterfall Ceremonial* taking place below the falls, with one order of business being the display and sale of native arts and crafts. Along with the Taos and Picuris Pueblos, Nambe is especially noted for the crafting of micaceous cooking and storage pots. But black and red carved decorative ware is also produced here, along with fine art pieces, fetishes and other wares. You'll see various

studios at roadside as you follow Nambe Creek toward the pueblo village. *Cloud Eagle Studio Gallery, Creations in Clay by Lonnie,* the *Guttierrez Studio,* and *Native American Heirlooms* by Pearl Talachy, are just some of the shop/galleries, indicating the renewed interest in the arts this pueblo now has after a dormant period of many years.

<u>Recreation</u> - *Nambe Falls Recreation Area* is the chief attraction of course. It's open 6 AM to 9 PM in summer, and 7 AM to 7 PM in winter. Closed November to March. Fishing for cutthroat and rainbow trout in Nambe Lake above the falls ($5 for adults for 10 catches/day, children $3 for 7 catches/day.) Season permits available. Non motorized boating is allowed on the lake, 14 feet or under, for $7/day. The park offers both picnicing ($5 per car) and camping ($7 first night, $4 each following night). Hiking and sightseeing $2 per person. Camping and picnic sites have grills, electric hookups, toilets and picnic tables. You can pay applicable fees and ask questions at the recreation area entrance. Nambe also offers bus tours to the other pueblos.

<u>Ceremonials</u> - The annual St. Francis of Assisi Feast Day is October 4, but other events take place too. Check with the Governor's Office for dates.

For more information contact: Nambe Ranger Station, Ph. (505) 455-2304; or Nambe Pueblo Governor's Office, Route 1, Box 117-BB, Santa Fe NM 87501.

*Touring The Pueblos*

## POJOAQUE and SANTA ANA

The old Pojoaque Pueblo lands are located on NM 84/285, 15 miles north of Santa Fe. Not much remains to define the original village except for low mounds among more modern dwellings. Pojoaque (means "water drinking place" in the Tewa tongue) largely abandoned its traditional lands back in 1890 following a smallpox epidemic. The population gradually decreased to but 40 members by the early 1930's, the residents living in other villages and off the reservation. Slowly but surely since then however - especially after the tribe regained much of its ancestral homeland - the population has increased, now numbering just over 200.

The present concentration of the tribe is in the *Pojoaque Pueblo Plaza* area, on the east side of NM 84/285 as you approach the junction with NM 502 from the south. Here you'll find the *Pojoaque Tourist Center and RV Park*. The tourist center includes an arts and crafts store with an impressive array of pottery, jewelry, weavings, paintings, sculptures and other items, especially by artists from Tewa speaking pueblos. Not much, if any, "souvenir"

*Touring The Pueblos*

quality goods are to be found here at this house of quality Indian-made wares.

Next door is an official state tourist center, also operated by the tribe, in which you will find a wide range of maps, area promotional brochures, travel, cultural and history books and publications relating to Indian Country, plus free information about the latest Indian doings. Nearby in the same large building complex is the *Poeh Center* - a cultural center and museum devoted to advancing and promoting the Pojoaque culture and that of the other Tewa speaking tribes. Poeh means "pathway," and refers to the traditional pueblo way of life, stressing the harmony which such a lifestyle brings. The finest in Indian paintings, sculpture, pottery and jewelry is on display here in a classy setting, and should not be missed

*Pojoaque Tourist Center Shop*

if you're anywhere near. The present museum is only temporary, as a new *Poeh Center* is abuilding at this writing, to include a museum having a permanent art collection, a gallery with traveling exhibits, and a training complex.

<u>SANTA ANA</u> - A second traditional pueblo whose physical traces have largely faded into obscurity is that of Santa Ana, located on NM 44, 8 miles northwest of Bernalillo (located among the Middle Rio Grande Pueblos). As with Pojoaque, nearly all of its people have moved to more modern homes on and off the reservation. Santa Ana craftpersons have revived ancient arts and craft traditions in the last couple of decades, and now produce pottery, woven belts, headbands, fine arts and jewelry items. You'll find these wares at the *Ta Ya Cooperative Association*, located at New Santa Ana, 2 miles east of Bernalillo off NM 313. *Ta Ma* is open 10 AM to 4:30 PM Tuesdays and Thursdays, and from noon to 4 PM Sundays.

Picnicing on Santa Ana lands can be enjoyed at the *Jemez Canyon Dam*, 5 miles out on the Jemez Canyon Dam Road. The *Valle Grande Golf Course* (27 holes) and the *Prairie Star Restaurant* are also operated by the tribe.

Both of these old Pueblo Indian villages of Pojoaque and Santa Ana have lost much of their physical identity, their people becoming more assimilated into the mainstream even as the people struggle to hang onto traditional ways. One wonders if in the end they will be counted among those other pueblo villages which once rose, thrived and ultimately disappeared as living entities. Some of those now extinct pueblos of the past were wondrous indeed.

## Touring The Pueblos

There was *Mesa Verde*, in Colorado. At the time Christ was born thousands of pueblo Indians dwelt in the flatlands of Mesa Verde, growing corn, squash and beans. There came a time when they began to build. They built dwellings now called Cliff Palace, Spruce Tree House, and Sun Temple, with towers, square cornered houses and round kivas. They were experts at adapting stone and mortar to fit the shape of hollowed-out cliffs. Style, beauty, safety and self defense - these were the qualities which emerged in the construction of all these dwellings. But the Indians lived at Mesa Verde for only about three centuries before they abruptly packed up and moved on. Was it the killer drought which occurred in the late 13th century which caused the mass exodus? Was it the ravages of nomadic Indian raiders? Maybe it was both, though no one knows for sure. The pueblos had no written language to record the pivotal events of their history.

There is the ruin of *Chaco Canyon* in northwest New Mexico, with its Pueblo Bonito ruin – largest "apartment house" in the world until late into the 19th century. There were 800 rooms and 5,000 people at Bonito, the complex rising five stories high. It took 100 years to complete the village, but these people too packed up and left, abandoning a once mighty citadel and thriving culture.

There is the ruined Pueblo village of *Tyuonyi* located in what has become Bandelier National Monument, near Los Alamos. The inhabitants came from Chaco Canyon, Mesa Verde and Canyon de Chelly to build this circular, four story high dwelling, with its four concentric walls and 400 rooms. It was – and still is – a pleasant area to reside in, with lush vegetation and a stream flowing between steep canyon walls. Yet these people too packed up and left.

## Pojoaque and Santa Ana

And there was the *Pecos Pueblo*, east of Santa Fe. It was one of the largest of the pueblos when Coronado visited in 1541. It had walls made of more modern sunbaked adobe bricks instead of rocks and mortar, and from its beginnings in about 1300 AD it held the promise of long survival, with its good croplands and adequate water supply. But it too met with calamity - the reasons for this one known all too well, since its demise occurred within the time of written history. Unabated attacks by the Comanches, and the ravages of smallpox spelled doom for the Pecos people. By 1800 there was but a handfull of Pecos left of the original 2500-plus. By 1838 only 17 souls remained. That's when the language-related Jemez tribe invited them to join their village, and there the Pecos descendants reside today. Like Mesa Verde, Chaco Canyon and Tyuonyi, this village too has been taken over by the National Park Service in order to protect what remains... All these ancient villages, plus those of Puye, Aztec, Po-Shu, Hovenweep and many others, are extinct villages, silent skeletans of what was. And now the ancient physical remains of Santa Ana and Pojoaque are fading to dust too. But the enemies of their survival aren't drought or attacks from marauding Indian tribes, or even disease. Their enemies are more the trademarks of modern industrial society - the ever powerful influences of change and progress.

If the physical presence of Pojoaque and Santa Ana seem to be slowly dissolving back into the earth whence they came, the members of these two tribes haven't melted into the mainstream quite yet. There are entities like the *Poh Center* mentioned above, whose mission is to

*Touring The Pueblos*

keep old tribal traditions alive. And both tribes continue to hold annual festivals on tribal lands, which tribal members often travel long distances to attend.

<u>Ceremonials</u> - Pojoaque has its annual Feast of Our Lady of Guadalupe on December 12, near the Pojoaque Pueblo Plaza. And there's the Annual Plaza Feast Day, held in the first week of August, when there is likely to be Indian, American and Spanish dancing, and food, plus lots of native arts and crafts on display.

About the only times that the gate to the Santa Ana Pueblo is open (located 10 miles northeast of Bernalillo on NM 44) is on its annual feast days of July 25 and 26; on January 1 and 6; on Easter Sunday; and on the days December 25 through 28. You'll find plenty of dancing, food, and arts and crafts wares on all these occasions.

For more information about these two pueblos contact: Governor's Office, Pueblo of Santa Ana, Star Route, Box 37, Bernalillo NM 87004. Ph. (505) 867-3301.

Governor's Office, Pueblo of Pojoaque, Route 11, Box 71, Santa Fe NM 87501. Ph. (505) 455-2278

# TESUQUE

You reach the Tesuque Pueblo by driving 9 miles north from Santa Fe on US 64-84. You'll see the entrance on the west side of the highway.

Highlight: *Historic row houses on village plaza.*

Tesuque (means "cottonwood tree plaza") is situated by the banks of the tree lined Tesuque River, and may have been inhabited as far back as the year 1200 AD. The pueblo is on the National Register of Historic Places for the very picturesque (though somewhat tumbledown) two-story row houses which border the central plaza. The hues of the adobe walls are those of pastel orange, beige and gray, and are striking in their sense of the old pueblo world. The small mission church, built in 1915 on the original site, is also quaint and photogenic, with its small bell tower and twin crosses. No fee for visiting, but the tribe requests that visitors not explore beyond the plaza area. A photo fee may be applicable during ceremonials (check with officials).

This small pueblo (population: 365) is noted as a very conservative one, and never mind the fact it's so close

*Touring The Pueblos*

to modern Santa Fe. (Tesuque is also just a stone's throw away from the famed Santa Fe Opera.) You can't miss Tesuque. It's trademark is Camel Rock, an ages-old sandstone likeness of a dromedary, sculpted by wind, rain and frost, located next to the tribally owned RV park. The camel sits there season after season, staring steadily northward, thinking of who knows what? He was there long before the time back in 1855 when then Defense Secretary Jeff Davis authorized $30,000 to be spent on a camel experiment. During the next two years some 77 of the beasts were imported to the southwest to see how they would fare as beasts of burden. Camels worked well in the deserts of the Middle East, so why not here? But they just didn't catch on. Maybe southwesterners weren't ready for camels.

*Tesuque Row House Complex*

*Tesuque*

<u>Shopping</u> - Tesuque artisans create both decorative and micaceous pottery, fine art, sculptures, miniatures, embroidery and other wares. Look for these items at *Duran's Pottery*, at *Teresa Tapia Pottery*, and at the convenience store next to the RV park.

<u>Recreation</u> -Tesuque owns and operates what may be the best tribally-owned RV park of them all. The *Tesuque Pueblo RV Campground* is located just north of Camel Rock, and has 63 full hookup RV spaces, plus a tent area. This all-season facility has showers, a laundry, a convenience store, and good on-site security. During the warmer months there is also a heated swimming pool and hot tub in operation. Full hookups include water, electric and sewer, and cost $15 daily for a couple, with $2 extra for additional persons. Children under 12 free. Weekly and monthly rates. Dry tent camping costs $12 per couple, with $2 for additional persons. Children free. For information call (505) 455-2467.

There is also *Tesuque Pueblo Bingo*, located across the highway from the RV park and a bit south. Open every night except Tuesday, starting at 5 PM, with an early bird special starting at 6:30. There is now a high stakes MegaBingo game. Bingo packages start at $5. There's a small bar at the parlor too. For details call (505) 984- or 1-800-85BINGO.

Horseback riding is offered through the *Camel Rock Ranch*. Call (505) 986-0408 for information.

<u>Ceremonials</u> - The annual San Diego Feast Day is November 12, when tribal dances, Indian food and arts and crafts displays can be enjoyed. Other annual events include Kings Day in January, a Corn Dance the first weekend in June, and Christmas celebrations.

*Touring The Pueblos*

For more information contact: Governor's Office, Tesuque Pueblo, Route 11, Box 1, Santa Fe NM 87501. Ph. (505) 983-2667.

# PART TWO

# MIDDLE
# RIO GRANDE PUEBLOS

## Touring The Pueblos

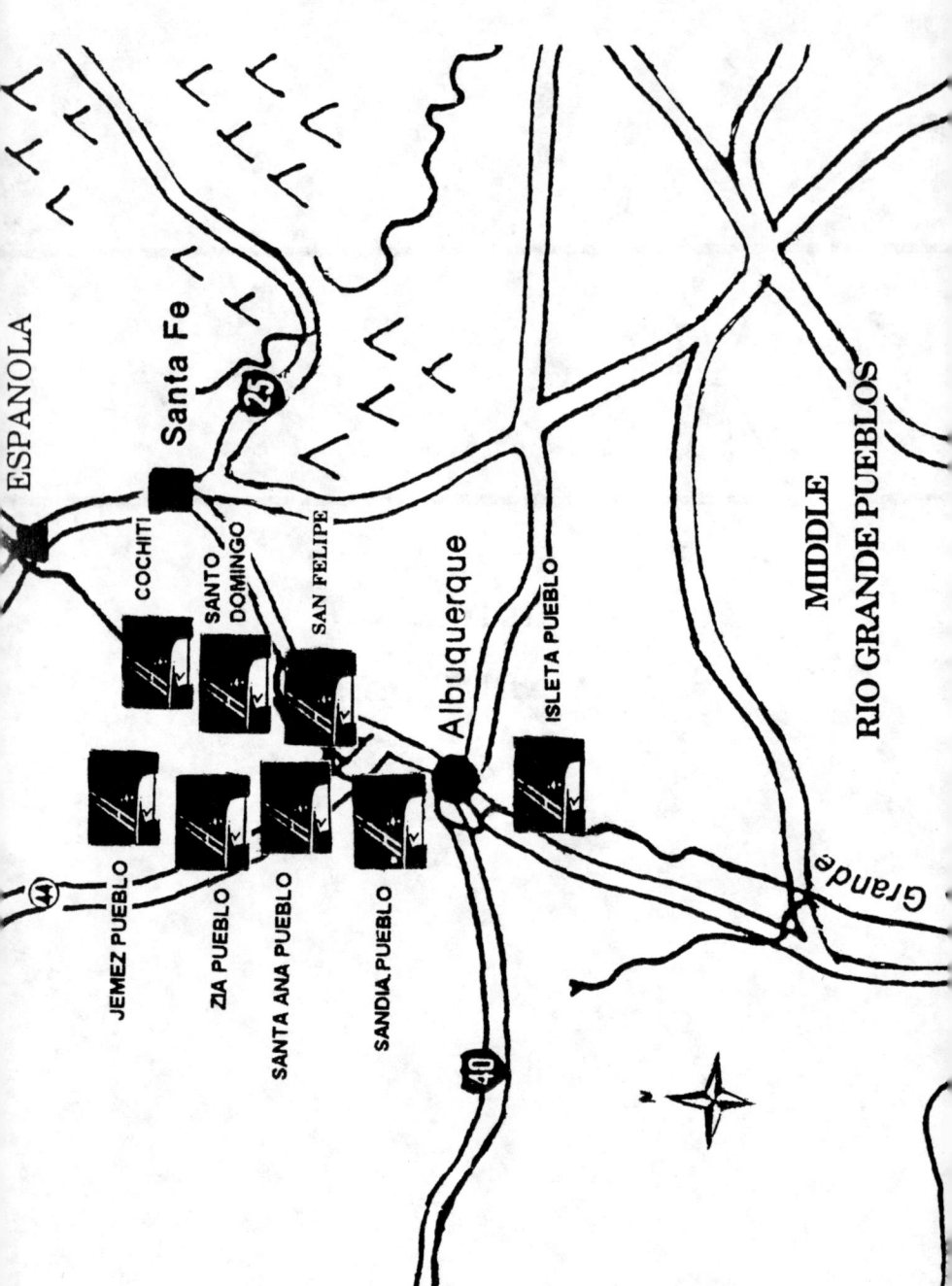

## COCHITI

The turn-off to Cochiti Pueblo is located 22 miles south of Santa Fe on I-25. Drive north 14 miles until you reach the access road.
   Highlights: *Storytellers and* Drum Making.
   As with the other Keres pueblos, Cochiti was friendly to the Spanish when they first arrived. But they too grew weary of the tributes exacted, the religious practices banned, and the servitude and false imprisonment. Thus, they participated vigorously in the Pueblo Revolt. Afterward they fled to more defensible locations atop Horn Mesa on the Pajarito Plateau, behind the present-day village. They were there until 1696, when de Vargas' soldiers, led by friendly Indian guides to the mesa top village, attacked the pueblo mercilessly, destroying it completely. It was never occupied again. No further retribution was exacted by the Spanish however, and the Indians returned to their home villages in peace.
   The present village of Cochiti (population: about 1,000) was established when the village's

## Touring The Pueblos

ancestors came down from pueblos in Frijoles Canyon on the Pajarito Plateau. Nothing physically spectacular about this medium size village today except for its location at the southern end of Cochiti Lake, which collects the flow of the Rio Grande as it flows out from between high, steep cliffs. An exploration of the pueblo (no fees, but no photography/sketching allowed) will lead you past two large round kivas with heavy *vigas* extending out; past weathered adobe dwellings intermixed with more modern structures; and past the golden-hued mission church built in 1628, with its heavy beam front facade and balcony. Weathered *hornos* are scattered here and there, and while you explore chances are good that you'll hear the sound of drums. The sound isn't from tribal festivities, but from the *testing* of drums. For this pueblo is noted for the making of quality traditional drums used in pueblo ceremonials. A sure sign of the pueblo's drum making activities is seen in the likenesses of drums painted on water tanks just north of the village. One charm of this village is the variety of hues seen on the exteriors of dwellings — pastel yellow. pink, beige, brown and orange hues.

Besides drum making, Cochiti is distinguished for the making of another unique Indian art and craft item: *storyteller figures*. Cochiti was the home of one of the "stars" of Indian arts and crafts, Helen Cordero. Her storyteller fame lives on today, and thrives throughout the Pueblo World. You'll find studios behind many a Cochiti "Crafts" sign which sees the creation of these colorful figurines.

The making of figurines goes far back in Cochiti history of course — to well before the Pueblo Revolt of 1680. Human and animal figurines have long been made of clay in the Pueblo World. Bird shaped pots

## Cochiti

with spouts shaped like beaks is one Cochiti trademark. When the railroad brought more and more travelers, the array of figurine designs expanded to meet the increasing demand. But the *storyteller figure* really put Cochiti on the modern arts and crafts map. It was in the year 1964 when Helen Cordero made her first storyteller, based on memories of childhood stories told to her by relatives. It served as the basis for a new and popular genre of potterymaking which was to spread well beyond Cochiti, delighting collectors, dealers and tourists alike. Helen Cordero's storytellers were to grace the cover of *National Geographic,* and take places of honor in museums like the *Heard* and the *Museum of International Folk Art,* among others. Not to mention numerous awards at Native American exhibits. Storytellers are exactly what the name implies: clay figurines which portray an adult Indian man or woman (or bear, frog, or other animal form nowadays) with mouth open in the act of speaking or singing, with children sitting or scrambling over him or her, or at the feet of the storyteller, listening raptly to the story being told. The adult figure often has its eyes closed for greater concentration. The adult always seems a bit larger than life compared to the children, who may number as many as 30.

    A storyteller starts in the mind of the individual potter, who draws on his (or her) sense of pueblo history, pueblo life, and individual experience, as one life source (the clay) is used to represent aspects of another life source, the living pueblo. As with a clay pot or bowl, a storyteller takes shape with a hollow center. In Cochiti's case clay gathered from the nearby Santo Domingo Pueblo is used. After the figure has been formed it is allowed to dry for several weeks before being meticulously sanded to a smooth texture, white slip added coat after coat, and finally vegetable paints used for markings and decoration. At the same time the "wee ones" – the children who are seen listening to what the storyteller is saying – are taking shape apart from the main figure, each one assuming a different stance and expression. The figures are appliqued to the main figure after firing. The completed figurine is then fired in the traditional way. As any storyteller afficianado will tell you, the artist at a particular pueblo will make these charming figurines embody the qualities which set the home pueblo apart from all others. This remains true even when certain potters stray from traditional practices to use commercial clays, acrylic paints, and electric kilns. (Traditionalists like Helen Cordero have maintained that a storyteller doesn't really come alive unless produced in the "old way.") More recently, Louis and Virginia Naranjo became the "stars" of Cochiti's storyteller tradition. Unlike traditional pottery, basketry, jewelry, and kachina making, however, storytellers were, from the start, produced for the tourist trade. The storyteller has become so popular that the genre has been broadened to include *miniature* storytellers only a couple of inches high. No commercial shops at the Cochiti Pueblo where you can buy these unique figurines, but you'll see many "Crafts" signs in front of residences where they can be bought. Buying direct from an artist may be the best way there is of buying Indian handmade crafts.

    The second craft which Cochiti is noted for is *drum making*. Not the kind of tom-toms used in frontier times to send messages, but the deeper, more resonant kind used in ceremonials. Several pueblos make drums, but Cochiti is preeminent. The process is rigorous and not very rewarding financially for the artist. But as with many pueblo endeavors it is the *doing* which counts. The drum maker first scouts the

## Cochiti

high country for a downed aspen tree with a suitable trunk. After getting it home he laboriously carves out the inner pulp to leave a drum shell. To this he attaches elk or cowhide which has been scraped bare of hair and then softened and stained. After the hide is attached to the shell it is usually painted according to the new owner's wishes. You'll find drums for sale at the annual *Santa Fe Indian Market*, at various pow-pows, and at the homes of various drum makers at Cochiti. Visit any pueblo ceremonial and you'll see these distinctive drums and hear their deep sonority as they establish the beat.

*Cochiti Storyteller*

*Touring The Pueblos*

<u>Recreation</u> – Not much in the way of recreation possibilities in the old pueblo itself, but there is no shortage at nearby *Cochiti Lake*, located on Cochiti ancestral lands. Cochiti Dam is listed as one of the world's largest earthfill dams, extending 5 miles across both the Rio Grande and Santa Fe River drainages. The lake is 7 miles long, with 21 miles of shoreline. It offers boating, fishing, picnicing, swimming and camping. The lake is stocked with largemouth bass, rainbow trout, walleye, crappie, bluegill and catfish (New Mexico fishing licenses required). No fees for day use hiking, picnicing, boating and sightseeing, but fees are applicable for camping at the two campgrounds. Covered shelters, grills, restrooms and electrical hookups are provided. Call (505) 242-8302 for further information.

The town of *Cochiti Lake* (on land leased from the tribe) is located just north of the dam, and offers an 18 hole golf course, tennis courts, dry dock, swimming pool and a small commercial center.

<u>Ceremonials</u> – The St. Buenaventure Feast Day is on July 14, with other doings on Christmas, New Years, Easter, and at other times on short notice.

For more information concerning Cochiti Pueblo contact: Governor's Office, P.O. Box 70, Cochiti Pueblo, NM 87072. Ph. (505) 465-2244.

## SANTO DOMINGO

You reach the Santo Domingo Pueblo by taking the Santo Domingo exit off I-25, about 25 miles south of Santa Fe.

<u>Highlight</u>: *Heishe necklaces.*

The site of the modern Santo Domingo Pueblo is the most recent of several riverside home sites for this pueblo, after moves made necessary by flooding of the Rio Grande. Back in history this Keresan speaking people resided at famous Chaco Canyon. Then they moved to the great pueblo of Mesa Verde, then to the Bandelier ruins in Frijoles Canyon, and finally here beside the Rio Grande. The Santo Domingos got along well with the Spanish when they first settled the area — enough so that the Spanish established a provincial headquarters at the pueblo, and built a large mission church. But by the time of the Pueblo Revolt the Santo Domingos' hospitality toward the Spaniards had worn thin. They joined spiritedly in the battle against the Spanish, to the extent of leaving three friars dead at the mission altar. The Santo Domingos were slow to warm up to the Spanish after the Reconquest, and to this day

## Touring The Pueblos

the tribe remains one of the most traditional and conservative, even though its location is and was part of that old historic byway, the Camino Real.

The pueblo village (population about 4,000) is made up of the typical flat roofed desert adobe buildings, interspersed nowadays with a smattering of prefab homes. A brilliant white-hued mission church sits at the head of the village plaza area, with turquoise blue and red geometrics and horse motifs on the facade and on the entranceway portal just in front of the church. Aged cronies in traditional shawls walk solemnly down the streets, while equally aged Santo Domingo men lean against the sides of buildings with colorful bandanas around their foreheads, talking quietly. Meanwhile their grandsons and daughters tear around in modern pickups, raising a cloud of dust.

Santo Domingo Indian Trading Post.

*Santo Domingo*

Three miles north of the pueblo (but still on reservation lands) is another attraction of note — fascinating enough to draw the interest of the likes of John F. Kennedy in 1962, of Red Skeleton, Jack Palance, and many another notable too. It's the *Santo Domingo Indian Trading Post*, of course, originally established in 1881 (rebuilt in 1921). You'll know you've arrived when you notice the "This Is It" sign out front of the aging brick building, and the 1950 Frazer Manhattan sedan rusting quietly in the sun, rain and winter cold. Inside you'll see an old style white trader-owned and operated Indian trading post gone berserk. There are some of the old trading post basics — grub, tack, yard goods, hardware — but mostly it's doodads, geegaws, and a cornucopia of curios which dazzle your eyes — some tacky, some quality-made, but all eye catching. No wonder the store has been the subject of feature stories over the years in publications such as *Life Magazine*, the *New Mexican*, the old *Look Magazine*, and others.

If most other pueblos are dependant on walk-in traffic for the sale of their arts and crafts items, Santo Domingos have always been noted as the best traveling salesmen. From the first their trademark goods have been beads and necklaces — a specialty which continues to this day. Their skill as traders equals or exceeds their skills at the making of heishe (shell), turquoise, coral, "liquid silver," and other types of beads and necklaces, in which their skill is consummate. In earlier days they would travel well worn sales routes to Navajo lands for silver, blankets and rugs, and to other pueblos for whatever they had to offer. In those earlier days the Santo Domingos had almost exclusive use of the famed Los Cerrillos turquoise mine nearby, and tended to dispense its treasures in ways which

*Touring The Pueblos*

benefited the tribe. Nowadays, Santo Domingo necklaces are seen all over the world. Here on the reservation you can find them at and around the *Cultural Center* just off the I-25 freeway entrance to the reservation, and at many shops in the pueblo at prices which tend to be more negotiable than at most pueblos. The Santo Domingos also make bird fetishes of turquoise and other materials. Pottery, too, is made here. Traditional designs go back to 1700 or before, with "simple geometrics" the name most often applied to their favorite decorative style.

<u>Shopping</u> – A walk through the old pueblo will reveal a goodly number of trading posts, shops and homes with crafts signs out front. The Santo Domingos, being instinctive traders, seem a bit more amenable to horse trading. Also at Santo Domingo are eateries where one can sample Indian cooked food from Mexican, American and Indian cuisines.

The aforementioned *Santo Domingo Trading Post* is an establishment with a full line of Indian made wares, including more than their fair share of souvenir quality items.

At the junction of I-25 and the Santo Domingo turn-off, the tribe has built their modern *Cultural Center*, with historical photos and artifacts, but also a gift area with a full range of Santo Domingo goods. Out front are booths where artists sell their own wares from table tops.

Finally, there is the *Santo Domingo Arts and Crafts Market*, conducted on Labor Day at the pueblo, featuring the work of a large number of Santo Domingo artists. Some of the best of Pueblo Indian dances are held at the same time, along with much in the way of homemade food, hot off the griddle.

## Santa Domingo

<u>Ceremonials</u> – The annual feast day is August 4, when hundreds of Santo Domingos mount one of the most impressive *Corn Dances* to be seen in the pueblo world. One of the reasons, no doubt, is that corn continues to be the tribe's most important agricultural crop.

For more information, contact: Governor's Office, Santo Domingo Pueblo, New Mexico. 87052. Ph. (505) 465-2214.

## Touring The Pueblos

*San Felipe hornos oven*

## SAN FELIPE

The San Felipe Pueblo is located about 10 miles north of Bernalillo, off I-25.

<u>Highlight</u>: *Ceremonial dances.*

Like Santo Domingo just to the north, San Felipe is located beside the meandering Rio Grande, and astride the famed *Camino Real*. This pueblo once had the only wagon bridge in western North America. Behind the pueblo rises Santa Ana Mesa, on which the tribe lived before moving down to riverside. The village (current population about 2,600) was founded in 1706, and may be the most conservative of the Keresan speaking pueblos. When you cross the river and drive its dusty streets you have a sense of time standing still. A horseman waters his mount in the shallows of the river. Horses and other livestock wander through the town undisturbed. No restaurants to be seen here, no stores, no trading posts. Just a lonely post office to show a link with the outside world. If any of the pueblo villages could be called sleepy, this one is it. The usual *horno* ovens are seen in yards bound by pole fences. Here and there is a cornfield, carefully fenced to keep livestock out. Off to the southeast the massive shoulders of the Sandia Mountains jut into the sky.

## Touring The Pueblos

It's a sleepy little village all right – except for certain eventful days and nights, that is. For on those special days and nights San Felipe undergoes a metamorphosis. It comes alive with ceremonial dances. The dances have made San Felipe notable in the pueblo world. Most significant are the *Green Corn Dance* (May 1), the *Corn Dance* (last weekend in June), and the *Buffalo Dance* (February 2). But there are others scheduled at short notice throughout the year.

Ceremonials have been a part of Pueblo Indian life ever since the earliest villages were established, and have become even more popular in the modern changing world. There are *Tableta Dances* (named for the shingle-like headdress worn by female dancers), often known as *Corn* or *Harvest Dances*, held especially at planting and harvest times, and meant to entreat the gods to provide rain and good planting. There are various animal dances – buffalo, elk, deer and others – held in supplication for good hunting and an abundance of meat and animal skin clothing. The *Buffalo Dance* is the most performed, liable to be held at any time of the year (instead of the winter months when most other animal dances are held). The buffalo hunt was important to the Rio Grande Pueblos in the old days. The dances can take on the aspects of profound and complex drama, especially when only a few dancers perform and interrelate as in a ballet, acting out themes of tragedy and death, of life and the reverence for life – both that of humans and of others of earth's inhabitants. There are also *Kachina Dances* in the Pueblo World, where masked male dancers assume a middleman role between kachina spirits and human beings (often not open to the public). A specialized but very impressive annual ceremonial is the *Shalako*, put

*San Felipe*

on by the Zunis in early fall. An all night affair, the dancers wear larger-than-life masks in a ritual meant to impress the Zuni gods. The Hopis have a wide range of cremonials, too, including the famed *Snake Dance* (often closed to the public), where, as in tradition, snake handling is an integral part of the ritual. Christian saint days provide an annual occasion for ceremonials at most pueblos, which combine pueblo tradition with Christianity. Easter is one such, when some events continue for days. The Christmas period is another hallmark ceremonial period.

Preparations for a ceremonial usually start well before the event, as costumes are made, dance steps polished, bread baked in *horno* ovens, and food prepared. In addition, arts and crafts items are readied for possible sale, not only by the pueblo hosting the dance, but by visiting members of other pueblos as well.

Drums are an integral part of the dance festivities, for the deep, hypnotic beat they provide. A chorus of singers – led by the older men of the tribe – carries the message of the dance in the native tongue. The dancers assemble in the plaza, all of them knowing exactly what is required of them. There are dances performed by children alone, and others performed by male and female adults, the long lines made up sometimes of hundreds of performers, keeping time to the heavy beat, the exuberance of color in the costumes a veritable flashing rainbow of changing hues. The outerwear is decidedly unconventional from the Anglo perspective. The male dancer, as an example, will probably be wearing some kind of stylized tribal mocassin on his feet, decoration below his knees in the form of colored yarn perhaps, with bells often adorning his ankles for additional flair.

## Touring The Pueblos

Seashells, turquoise armbands, sashes, animal skins, bow guards, and other acoutrements are added in various places, with a gourd rattle in hand to add to the statement to be made. Around the plaza the lines — often two at a time — move forward then back, then in a sidestepping motion. It's a glimpse of the past as it was perhaps 1,000 years ago, except that the modern version is without a doubt more saturated with color. This is a religious event of course. The dances are meant both to honor the supernatural spirits which guide the dancers' destinies, and also to beseech them for an abundant life. In the ceremonials honoring Christian personages, the occasion is more solemn, with costumes more subdued, as thanks and beseechings are made to the God brought by the Spaniards 450 years ago.

All the pueblos conduct their own ceremonials, as a means of reconstituting tribal identity and carrying on tradition. Even when tribal members have lost some of the strength of their ties to ancestral homelands, they still make it a point to return home during ceremonial occasions. Check with the

*San Felipe Pueblo*

## San Felipe

Governor's Office at any given pueblo for upcoming events. Most are open to the public, but not all. Since they are religious occasions, most pueblos (except the Tewa villages of Santa Clara, San Ildefonso, San Juan and Nambe) don't allow photography, sketching or video recording during ceremonials. Acoholic beverages are generally banned from all pueblo lands. Check with the individual tribe if you have questions.

San Felipe is not noted as a hotbed of arts and crafts activity. However, there has been a resurgence of interest in traditional forms in recent years, as heishe and turquoise jewelry are being made once again, along with storyteller figures and other arts and craft forms.

No fee to wander the dusty streets of this village, but no photography/sketching allowed. No eating places, trading posts or recreational opportunities to speak of here, but there are several artists who sell their output from their homes. Check for signs. You'll find much in the way of arts and crafts, food, and something truly unusual in the way of entertainment, however, at San Felipe ceremonials.

For further information contact: Governor's Office, P.O. Box "A", San Felipe Pueblo, NM. Ph. (505) 867-3381.

## Touring The Pueblos

## ZIA

The Zia Pueblo is located 17 miles northwest of Bernalillo, just off NM 44.

<u>Highlight</u>: *Status as birthplace of New Mexico state symbol.*

Zia is a small pueblo now (populatiion just over 700) but in the glory days back in the 16th and 17th centuries it was one of the largest of the Rio Grande Pueblos, boasting a population of over 6,000. The settlement came into being around 1250, and eventually grew to have eight plazas with well built dwellings painted in lavish colors. But slowly, irrevocably, the pueblo declined. Relentless attacks by Navajos and other raiders, along with the ravages of small pox and other European diseases, decimated the population, leaving but 100 Zias by the late 19th century. Since then, however, there has been slow but steady population growth.

The entire village was razed to the ground at the time of the 1680 Revolt, so not much remains of the traditional village. If it hadn't been for the insistence of Diego de Vargas – the Spanish commander who

## Touring The Pueblos

reconquered the pueblos in 1692 – maybe Zia never would have been rebuilt. A dirt road winds around to the brow of the hill-top village, past stock pens, old wagon parts, solitary cottonwoods, and past the usual simple, flat roofed dwellings, some with that ancient symbol of the pueblos – the pinon pole ladder – leaned against a wall. Near the top is the simple square- built mission church with its thick beige colored adobe walls with a white facade and simple bell tower. Unfortunately for visitors, the doors are usually locked except during services.

One of the most noticeable aspects of this pueblo is the yellow-beige water tower which rises behind the village. Upon its curving surface you'll note the "Zia" sun symbol – the emblem which became New Mexico's state symbol, and which is found everywhere in the state. It makes up the field of the New Mexico state flag, decorates New Mexico vehicle license plates, and accents many another New Mexico logo. What you see is a red circle around a stylized yellow center, with sets of four narrow red rays extending out at the four points of the compass, all in a bright yellow background. Those are the original hues, but the variations on the theme are endless. It is here, at the Zia Pueblo, where the symbol was born. There had been two other state flags in New Mexico history, but neither seemed to catch the spirit of the state very well back in the 1920's. To remedy this lack the Daughters of the American Revolution sponsored a search for a new flag design in 1925. An anthropology buff named Dr. Harry Mera put forth a flag based on the unique design he'd seen on a handmade Zia pot of the late 19th century. The design seemed to capture the importance of the sun in the southwest, and of the necessary harmony between all living things, as seen in traditional pueblo philosophy.

The Zia motif won out over all the other designs offered, and so history was made. (The original pot with the Zia sun symbol now resides at the School of American Research in Santa Fe.)

Beyond the hilltop village, Indian Routes 78 and 79 lead out into the Zia Pueblo's 190 square mile reservation, taking in picturesque parts of the Sierra Naciemente Mountains and the Pajarito and Jemez Plateaux. The scenic vistas are inspiring enough to capture the attention of Hollywood in the making of diverse media productions. Zia actively solicits on-location business from film makers. With permission, visitors can wander the colorful back roads of the reservation at their leisure.

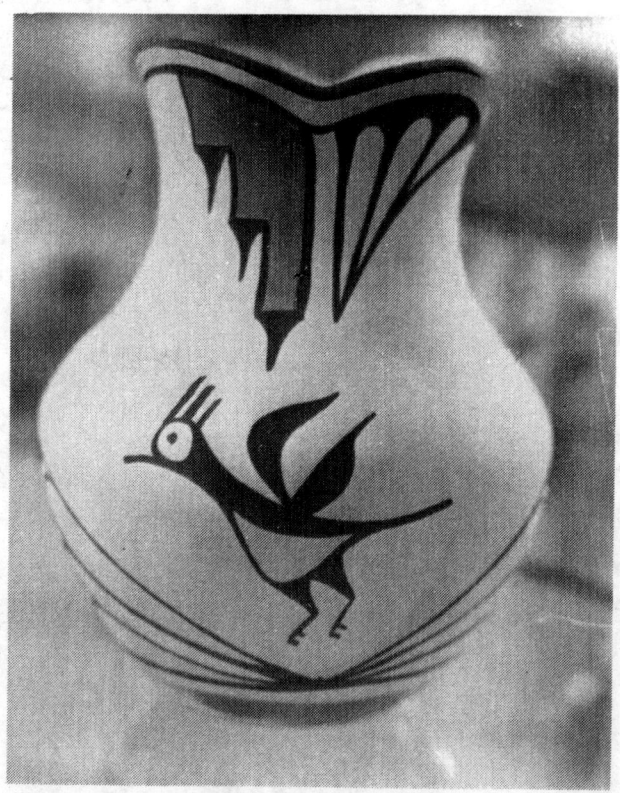

*Zia Pottery with "Zia bird"*

*Touring The Pueblos*

Near the entrance of this small, Keresan speaking pueblo, you'll see a complex of buildings on the right which include the tribal governor's offices, a small market and the *Cultural Center*. In the Cultural Center are historical photos and displays of stone sculptures, beadwork, figurines and pottery for sale. Pottery is the tribe's arts and crafts specialty – one they've practiced for centuries. Zia has never been big on crop growing due to the limited amount of arable land, but their pottery has provided a secure basis for trading with other tribes for necessary agricultural and other products. A famous pottery hallmark is the *Zia Bird* – a stylized road runner (the road runner bird is important in Zia mythology). You'll see the *Zia Bird* on pots in collections and on pottery shelves across the country and beyond. The double rainbow is another well known Zia motif. Zia pottery is tempered by using ground basalt (found especially in this area) making it – according to some – the hardest of all pueblo pottery. Fine art painting with oils and watercolors is also done at Zia, often with considerable skill.

<u>Recreatiion</u> – The primary recreation opportunity here is that of fishing. Trout and catfish can be hooked at *Zia Lake*, a year- around fishing hole located on the north side of the Jemez River, 2 1/2 miles west of the pueblo. Fees for fishing at the 30 acre lake are $4 per adult for a limit of eight fish per day.

<u>Ceremonials</u> – Annual feast day is August 15, but there are also festival days on Easter Sunday and Christmas, with an Indian pow-wow taking place on Memorial Day.

For more information contact: Governor's Office, Pueblo of Zia, General Delivery, San Ysidro NM 87052. Ph. (505) 867-3304.

## JEMEZ

You reach the Jemez Pueblo by taking NM 44 north from Bernalillo for 22 miles to San Ysidro, then turning right on NM 4. The pueblo is 5 miles north.

Highlights: *Beautiful setting; Old tribal ruins of Guisewa nearby.*

The pueblo sits in some of the most picturesque scenery of any of the pueblos. Red veined cliffs, anvil edged mesas, high tablelands and steep cliffs abound in this Colorado Plateau country. Conquistador Juan de Onate found the area so inviting back in the late 1500's that he made Jemez his provincial capitol. The hot springs located at the former pueblo village of Giusewa, 13 miles north of the present Jemez village, made the area even more inviting. In 1621 Fray Zarate Salmeron set out to convert the Indians to Christianity, and built a magnificent church – *San Jose de La Jemez* – near the hot springs, and looked forward to a good missionary effort. But problems developed here in Paradise. The area bordered hostile Apache and Navajo lands, and their raids were unrelenting. Droughts were also a continuing problem, even though the Jemez River flows through the valley. The 1640's were especially hard, and finally the village of Giusewa had to be totally abandoned, the inhabitants moving south to the location of the present Jemez Pueblo. As with the other pueblo tribes, the Jemez were reluctant subjects of the Spanish colonial empire. Involuntary servitude, harsh punishments, and the disruption of traditional ways, led the Jemez to join energetically in the Pueblo Revolt of 1680. Expecting retribution at the time of the Reconquest, the Jemez fled to a more defensible location on a nearby mesa top, where they estabIlished a new village. Meanwhile the Jemez set about attempting a new revolt to roust the Spanish. But Diego de Vargas – the reconqueror of pueblo lands – reacted to the defiance with vengeance. He defeated the Jemez on the top of San Diego Mesa by using overwhelming force. Tribal members fled to take refuge with the Apaches, Navajos and Hopis – but not before some Jemez threw themselves from the tops of cliffs to their deaths rather than risk capture. It was years before Jemez Pueblo was again reconstituted, its numbers reduced to a mere 300. Even after the Europeans and missionaries did make accomodations to the Indians, the psychological climate continued to be an uneasy one between Jemez and Spaniard. A history of violence has a way of projecting its dark fruits far into the future.

    Today the peace and serenity of the Towa speaking Jemez Pueblo belies its strife-torn past. The 1900 inhabitants go about their agrarian, small business and craftmaking lives in peace, in a culture which draws elements from both traditional and mainstream roots. The colors of private dwellings are darker and redder in hue than at other pueblos, reflecting the coloration of the surrounding landscape.

*Jemez*

*Guisewa Mission Church ruins at Jemez State Monument.*

*Touring The Pueblos*

More horses are in evidence here – a legacy, perhaps, of an intensive one-time alliance with the horse-addicted Navajos. You'll see sheepskins on fences, old farming implements rusting quietly through the seasons, and hear roosters crowing and turkeys gobbling. Check with tribal administration before exploring this pueblo. No photography/sketching allowed

Thirteen miles up the road is *Jemez State Monument*, which is the abandoned remains of that other Jemez village of the past – *Guisewa* (pronounced Gee-Say-Wa), which denotes the hot springs in the area. Nearby are the remnants of that once magnificent church of *San Jose de la Jemez*, with its massive stone and clay walls. A Visitor Center houses exhibits which tell the story of this village that had thrived for 200 years before the Spanish arrived, and which then took only a couple of decades to become a ghost town.

What a transformation it must have been for the local Jemez people when the friars arrived. Scores of the men were put to work building the church (one of the largest in the pueblo world at the time). There were no architects or construction engineers, so the church was built largely from the memories the friars had of Spanish churches, with a great deal of innovation thrown in. Up to a dozen of the locals were employed full time to help the two friars keep the church operating. Out in the fields new crops (to the Indians) of wheat, grapes, fruit and chile were being grown. At the same time, horses, mules, burros, chickens, goats and sheep – also new to the Indians – were being introduced to the Pueblo people. And of course there was the new religion, totally at odds with that of Pueblo tradition. All in all it had to be a culture shock of major

## Jemez

proportions – one experienced by all of the Pueblo tribes.

Jemez State Monument is open 9:30 AM to 5:30 PM from May 1 to September 15; 8:30 AM to 4:30 PM from September 16 to April 30. Admission is $2 for adults.

The Jemez were diligent and skilled potters before the Pueblo Revolt, but that event proved disastrous to the longstanding pottery tradition. The craft remained in a state of suspended animation after the Revolt and until the mid 1960's, when potter Helen Cordero (of Cochiti Pueblo) reinvented the storyteller figure. This engaging pottery specialty spread to other pueblos, including Jemez, in a remarkably short time. Now Jemez creates its full share of storytellers and other forms of figurative pottery. General potterymaking has also seen a revival here, with strong geometrics on a tan background a Jemez trademark. The surrounding hills offer clay in hues ranging from white to vivid reds to ochre, which are used to produce striking redware and polychrome pottery in a variety of shapes.

Shopping – Pottery, fine sculptures, mocassins, drums, jewelry, and other items can be bought directly from artists at homes displaying craft signs, at shops located on NM 4 through the village, and at a small general store near the north end of town. On weekends the place to go for arts and crafts, and for home-made Indian foods, is the *Red Rock Scenic Area*, on the highway two miles north of the village. This collection of permanent selling booths is also the location of the *Towa Arts and Crafts Show*, an annual event taking place every Memorial Day.

Recreation – A notable recreation opportunity at the Jemez Pueblo is fishing. About a dozen pueblos offer fishing to visitors (with no state license required), and in this Jemez excels. As with the other pueblos, stocker trout six to nine inches in length come from regional hatcheries, with some larger ones two to four pounds in weight planted too. Catfish and bass are two other resident species in most pueblo ponds. Jemez has two pond complexes: the *Holy Ghost Springs Recreation Area*, off NM 44, 18 miles north of San Ysidro (watch for a sign on the east side of the highway), open 7 AM to 7 PM, Wednesday through Sunday; and the *Dragon Fly Recreation Area*, 5 1/2 miles further north, on the west side of the highway. The Holy Ghost area has three good size ponds, one of which is restricted to flies and lures only. Fees (paid to the on-duty ranger) are $5 for adults for eight keepers, $3 for kids under 8. A platform for handicapped fishermen is located at the middle lake at Holy Ghost. Call (505) 834-7359 for further information on fishing, and also on limited hunting opportunities.

<u>Ceremonials</u> – A *Corn Dance* is held on the *Feast Day of San Diego* on November 12, when more arts and crafts and food are avaiilable. August 2 is the date for another annual feast day – the *Pecos Feast* – to commemorate that day in 1838 when the last remaining members of the Pecos tribe left their ancestral pueblo and moved to Jemez forever.

For further information contact: Tribal administrator, P.O. Box 100, Jemez Pueblo, NM 87024. Ph. (505) 834-7359.

# SANDIA

The Sandia Pueblo is located 13 miles north of Albuquerque, just off NM 313.

<u>Highlights:</u> *Recreation and Shopping*.

After the Pueblo Revolt of 1680 most of the residents of Sandia fled west to take refuge with the Hopis in Arizona. It wasn't until the mid 1700's that Sandia became full reestablished. Sandia has become more assimilated with the mainstream than most pueblos, though its people still hold fervently to old religious practices and dance energetically for rain during the annual St. Anthony's Feast Day on June 13. Not much Old Pueblo flavor to be seen when you visit this small village (population: 325), although the old mission church is picturesque, and the vague remains of the original village (established about 1300 AD) are still discernable near the present church. OK to explore this small pueblo, but no photography/sketching allowed.

A sidelight of interest is the *Sandia Tram* – longest tram in the world – where gondolas pass over leased Sandia lands on their way to the magnificent crest of the Sandia Mountains, where one can feast on the view at the same time as he can feast on good food

## Touring The Pueblos

at two restaurants.

    _Shopping_ – One feature setting Sandia apart from other pueblos is *Bien Mur Indian Market Center,* located just east of the Interstate 25-Tramway intersection at the northern edge of Albuquerque. Bien Mur is the largest of the pueblo reservation-based Indian arts and crafts retail establishments, devoted to selling Indian wares from the pueblos and other Indian groups. Bien Mur was established in the mid 1960's to accomodate a buying public which has become more and more interested in Indian arts and crafts. On the main floor and upstairs mezzanine the store offers the full range of Indian-made wares, from fine Zuni and Hopi turquoise and silver jewelry, to pottery fashioned according to each tribal specialty, to kachina dolls, Cochiti storytellers, Santo Domingo heishe, Navajo rugs, fine art paintings, sculptures, weavings, fetishes, and figurines from virtually all of the pueblos and other tribes as well. There is also a full range of books on Native Americana, crafts, and regional travel. Bien Mur is open Monday-Saturday from 9 AM to 5:30 PM; Sunday from 11 AM to 5 PM. Call (505) 821-5400 for more information.

    Why the surge in interest in Indian-made arts and crafts? There are a number of reasons. The modern age is one of assembly line production and uniform styling. With mass production comes affordable prices, true. But there's also a down side – a decrease in uniqueness of styling, artistic beauty, individuality, creative flair, and pride of ownership. Not to mention quality of workmanship. Handmade wares remedy these deficiencies on all counts when crafted by accomplished artists. In the case of Indian-made wares an additional bonus is the invisible bond which takes place between the purchaser and the

## Sandia

person and culture of the artist. It's a bond, a link which extends by definition back through the centuries. The factor of *tradition* is an important factor making Indian-made wares so much in demand these days. It's a tradition which bonds the Indian to his ancestral lands, one which gives homage to Mother Earth and all her creations, and one which embraces the "old ways" of craftmaking in preference to modern mass production methods and throw-away goods. In pottery the tradition is seen in the Acoma Indian's use of age-old Mimbres designs, in San Ildefonso Pueblo's ancestor-based black-on-black pottery, in the venerable micaceous pots of the Picuris, Taos and Nambe Indians; and in the inspiration drawn from old Sityatki designs by Hopi potters. In silver and turquoise jewelry the tradition is seen in symbols from a rich mythology. The symbols speak of ancient kachina spirits, of rain for crops, of storm clouds and lightning, of parrots, coyotes, buffalo and elk, of the frets, stripes, diamonds and other geometrics seen in formations of buttes, canyonlands and the Painted Desert. Even more fundamental and traditional are the methods used – methods involving the age-old potterymaking techniques of coiling, hand shaping, home firing and vegetable paints; in the methodical, often painstaking handworking steps involved in turning plain sheets of silver and uncut stones into jewelry items that both enchant the eye and stand the artistic test of time. These are the connections the buyer of Indian handmade items makes, and which have made these wares so much in demand... And which has seen the upsurge in the numbers of Native American artists, and in marketing venues like Bien Mur.

   Recreation – *Sandia Lakes Recreation Area*, located on NM 313 just north of Tramway/4th Street,

## Touring The Pueblos

*Sandia Lakes Recreation Area*

offers a number of recreation opportunities. Pond fishing offers the chance of catching rainbow trout, largemouth bass and catfish ($8 for adults, $6 for seniors, and kids under 5 free, for 8 keepers). Hours are 6:30 AM to about dusk, with a bait/tackle shop at the site. Snack foods available. There are shelters, a playground, barbecue pit, volleyball court, and nature trails. If you don't want to fish you can use these other facilities for $2 per person, under 5 free. The recreation area is open all year. For further information call (505) 897-3971.

For horse riding enthusiasts there's *Sandia Trails,* located just north of where 4th Street meets 2nd Street NW. You can ride scenic horse trails for $15/hr, or pay $20 for the 1 1/2 hours it takes to ride the longest trail. Reservations are recommended. The stables are open generally from 9:30 AM to 4:30 PM daily. Call (505) 898-6970 for reservations.

## Sandia

*Sandia Bingo* is a major bingo parlor, operating 24 hours a day, 7 days a week. You'll find it just north of Tramway Blvd on the west side of Interstate 25, on the northern edge of Albuquerque. Access is from Tramway. Look for the sign as you proceed west on Tramway. The parlor features MegaBingo, Las Vegas Bingo, Video Bingo, and pull tab gambling. There's a concession stand too. Call (505) 897-2173 for general information, and (505) 898-0852 for the Jackpot Hotline.

<u>Ceremonials</u> – *St. Anthony's Feast Day* falls on June 13, but there are other doings throughout the year as well.

For further information contact: Governor's Office, Sandia Pueblo, P.O. Box 6008, Bernalillo, NM 87004. Ph. (505) 867-3317.

*Touring The Pueblos*

# ISLETA

Isleta Pueblo is 12 miles south of Albuquerque, just off I-25. Watch for a sign.

<u>Highlight</u>: *Distinctive pottery.*

Isleta Pueblo is the southernmost of the Middle Rio Grande Pueblos, established around 1300 AD. The name Isleta – "Little Island" – is said to come from the pueblo's appearance when the Rio Grande flooded in the old days and swirled completely around the slightly higher ground of the village. The fertile, well watered soil gave this pueblo an early reputation for bountiful fruits and produce. The village – population about 3,500 – continues to be one of the most prosperous of all the pueblos.

Isleta has always had the reputation of being the one most friendly to the early Spaniards. It's true that the Isletans did not turn on the Spanish settlers during the 1680 Revolt as did the others. But when Antonio de Otermin returned a year later in a first feeble attempt at reconquest, he found the Isletans decidedly unfriendly, and even hostile. A battle ensued. The pueblo was defeated and the pueblo razed to the ground in punishment for their defiance. Otermin returned to

*Touring The Pueblos*

El Paso then, taking with him 375 of the Isleta natives. It wasn't until 1709 that Isleta became firmly reestablished.

Today, Isleta remains in the same location as in the earliest days, just south of the old crossing of the western branch of the *Camino Real* over the Rio Grande. The old church of St. Augustine is at the northern edge of the central plaza, where on the feast day of September 4 a wooden sculptural likeness of St. Augustine is paraded and given homage. The narrow, unpaved streets wind out and around from the central plaza area. You'll find that many of the flat, brown, beige and white adobe dwellings are built to include sections of the more ancient weatherbeaten walls of history.

Portions of the old walls also remain in the impressive St. Augustine Mission Church with its three bell towers. Originally established in 1613 – one of the oldest mission churches still functioning in the U.S. – it too tumbled largely into ruin after the Pueblo Revolt. But with the return of the Spanish came a rebuilding effort, which was finally completed in 1716. Inside you'll find a single long nave running between thick adobe walls, the roof supported by large and rugged *vigas*. At the front is a colorful altar, and on the walls centuries-old religious paintings. There's a small museum through a door to the right of the altar. The beige-gold outside walls of the church glow richly in the early morning light. As you wander the narrow streets of this 700 year old village you see *horno* ovens – often in pairs – decorating private yards, the smell of fresh cooked Indian bread often floating in the air.

Potterymaking is the main craft of the Isletas. Early on (late 1800's) black and red painted whiteware was produced here and offered to passengers of trains

*Isleta*

stopping in nearby Albuquerque. But the craft has matured since then, and new designs based on more enduring traditional styles are produced with high quality. Indeed, Isleta is home to one potter who has reached "name" status in the pueblo pottery world. Her name is Stella Teller, and a trademark of her white slipped ware is the subtle but striking gray tone she achieves in colored bands and accents. The frequent inletting of turquoise pieces into her vessels is another Teller feature. It was in the late 1800's when political differences in the Laguna Pueblo to the west drove many of the Lagunas to a refuge here in Isleta. Thus the Isleta potterymaking tradition has been influenced by the older Laguna tradition, which in turn was influenced by the nearby Acoma Pueblo. In the arts and crafts, as in other things, the various pueblos continue to influence one another. The Isletas also

*St. Augustine Mission Church*

## Touring The Pueblos

make storyteller figures – a craft form which saw its roots in the tradition started by Helen Cordero of Cochito Pueblo. Isleta craft workers also fashion a variety of engaging figurines.

<u>Shopping</u> – Arts and craft items are for sale at shops on the pueblo plaza, and at the homes of numerous artists – including Stella Teller – who have craft signs outside their homes. You'll find these artists both in the old pueblo and in several satellite villages.

<u>Recreation</u> – *Isleta Lakes* provides a rich opportunity for recreation – that of fishing and camping. This recreation area is reached by taking Exit 215, 12 miles south of Albuquerque and turning south on NM 47. The complex of three lakes is just down the road from the turnoff. The fishing is for trout, bass and catfish, and costs $5 for adults for eight keepers per day, and $2.50 for kids under 12 for four keepers. There's a bait/tackle shop at the site, where you can pay necessary fees.

Another recreation opportunity is the *Isleta Bingo Parlor,* located on NM 47 just south of I-25. Doors open at 5 PM, with an Early Bird Special at 6:45. Regular bingo starts at 7:15, and lasts until about 10 PM. The bingo hall features good cafeteria style food. Call (505) 869-2614 for details.

<u>Ceremonials</u> – The pueblo hosts two annual feast days, honoring St. Augustine. The one on August 28 is called the "Big Feast," while the one on September 4 is locally referred to as the "Little Feast." There are several other events throughout the year too, the exact dates established at short notice.

For further information contact: Governor's Office, P.O. Box 1270, Isleta NM 87022. Ph. (505) 869-3111.

# PART THREE

## WESTERN PUEBLOS

## Touring The Pueblos

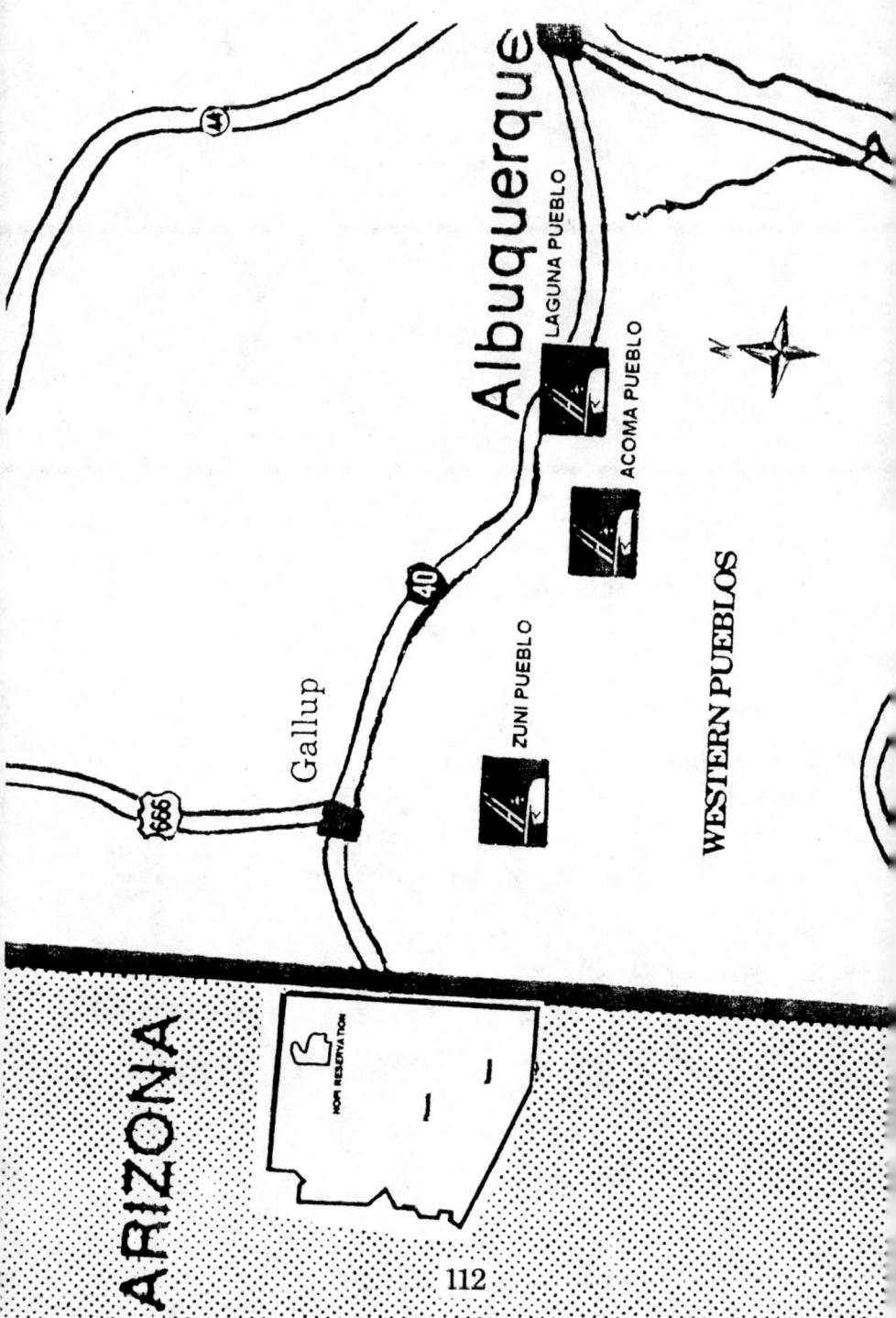

## LAGUNA

The Laguna Pueblo is located about 45 miles west of Albuquerque, astride Interstate 40. Watch for a sign.
Highlight: *St. Joseph Mission Church.*
Railroad tracks run parallel to Interstate 40, and in the old days when the iron horse first came to the west, the tracks led right through Laguna Pueblo – one of the first pueblos which railway passengers could visit without ever leaving the train.
Laguna is the most recently established of the pueblos, founded officially on July 4, 1699. Laguna could be called the "refugee pueblo," since it was started largely by refugees from other tribes, fleeing from the Spanish Reconquest. Transplanted refugees in the Hopi lands, too, returned to help swell the population, as did those residents of the Acoma Pueblo (on whose original lands the Laguna Pueblo rests) who had originally fled there. There were also refugees from the Zia, Sandia, San Felipe and Zuni Pueblos, making it truly a multi-tribal entity. Four different language groups were involved, which made

adjustments to life in the new pueblo even more difficult.

In fact there are distinct language differences among the various pueblo tribes. The Zunis speak Zuni, but it's the only tribe which does so. The Hopis also have their own tongue. The pueblos of Zia, San Felipe, Santa Ana, Cochiti, Santo Domingo, Laguna and Acoma speak Keresan. Taos, Sandia and Isleta speak Tiwa, while Santa Clara, San Ildefonso, San Juan, Pojoaque, Nambe and Tesuque speak Tewa, a language very similar to one spoke by the Plains Indian Kiowa tribe. The Jemez Pueblo speaks Towa – the last remaining tribe to do so. To make it even more complex, there are distinct differences in dialect among tribes speaking the same basic lingo.

The diversity of Laguna's cultural background is suggested by the fact that the tribe is made up of six different villages (including Old Laguna), spread over many square miles of arid desert arroyos and dunes near the San Jose River. Each village tends to have its own slant on ceremonials, and its own dates when ceremonials take place. The residents go about their business of growing agricultural products on fairly productive farmland. In former days Laguna was home to one of the largest uranium mines in the country.

There isn't a great sense of history to be found from a tour of the old pueblo of Laguna, except perhaps for a visit to the *St. Joseph Mission Church* – the highlight attraction of Old Laguna. The brilliant white facade of the church makes it stand out from the earthen colored buildings which surround it. The church is situated near the top of a knoll, and it stands to be the most seen mission church of all the pueblo churches, since it catches the eyes of millions of

*Laguna*

St. Joseph Mission Church at Old Laguna Pueblo.

## Touring The Pueblos

passersby on nearby Interstate 40. When you step through the ancient carved wooden door of this church you'll notice a sharp decline in temperature if it's warm outside. The floor is of packed earth, and there are two rows of wooden pews centered on a single aisle running to the altar at the front. The altar itself was hand carved by the Indians from pine logs, then painted by them. Behind the altar is a marvelous set of paintings. On the right is a portrait of Santa Barbara, patroness against thunder, lightning, firearms and sudden death. On the left is a painting of St. John Nepomucenez, venerated as patron of water (important in this arid land), and the seal of confessions. In the center is a painting of the Blessed Trinity. Above the altar on the ceiling is a painting on an animal hide with symbols representing the rainbow, sun, moon and stars, surrounded by Christian symbols in a diplomatic intermingling of Indian traditional religion and Christianity. In the ceiling of heavy timbered *vigas* is a herringbone pattern of cedar twigs. Along both walls from back to front are hand carved bas relief scenes in miniature, of wood, representing the "stations of the cross" – the sufferings of Christ on his way to Calvary. Below the carvings are painted Indian motifs in orange, black and white. There are other paintings and artwork too, in this compact but picturesque church. You'll find the doors unlocked most of the time, with visitors welcome – contrary to some other pueblo churches where the doors are kept locked. If only these thick adobe walls could talk! It is interesting that, in addition to its religious role, the church served as an administration building, as a stable, and as a lodging place for Puebloans fleeing marauding Apaches and Navajos. The thick adobe walls have also sheltered the likes of Kit Carson, Billy the Kid, and many another

## Laguna

famous and notorious personage.

<u>Recreation</u> – There is fishing at the *Paguate Reservoir* for bass and trout. You can obtain permits and directions at the Wildlife Conservation Office. Hiking, camping and picnicing facilities are available at nearby Mt, Taylor (off reservation lands).

<u>Ceremonials</u> – Check with pueblo offices for times and dates of ceremonials occurring in the various satellite villages. The most important are the *St. Joseph Feast Day* (the original feast day) held at Old Laguna on March 19; *St. John's Feast Day* on June 24; a more modern *St. Joseph's Feast Day* on September 19; and festivities at Christmas time.

For further information contact: Pueblo of Laguna, P.O. Box 194, Laguna, New Mexico 87026. Ph. (505) 552-6654.

*Touring The Pueblos*

## ACOMA 'SKY CITY'

You can reach the Old Acoma Pueblo ("People of the White Rock") by turning south from Paraje, 50 miles west of Albuquerque; or by turning south from McCartys, 12 miles further west.

<u>Highlights</u>: *Magnificent setting; Thin walled pottery.*

South from McCartys (the most scenic route) you drive across high desert terrain, the road winding past ancient stone dwellings, adobe ruins, and cornfields, then into juniper and pinon studded rolling hills with grazing horses visible on distant knolls. Finally you round a curve at the top of a high mesa and there it is below you – an almost mythic scene. Great buttes rise from a wide valley floor, their sculpted red and beige heights casting long shadows out behind the sun. Off to the southeast lies Enchanted Mesa, where according to legend, a mother and daughter were stranded after a violent rainstorm which washed out the only way down. With the trail gone, the two finally threw themselves off the cliff to avoid a long and painful starvation.

## Touring The Pueblos

You'll spot the star attraction – the Acoma "Sky City" – when you turn your gaze a bit further toward the south. The ancient pueblo is perched on top of a high mesa, its ancient adobe buildings almost blending in with the cliffs. You descend into the valley, and the closer you get to the soaring mesa on which the "city" is built, the more wondrous it seems. A complete Indian village of stone and adobe walled dwellings perched up there in the sky, splendid appearing, ethereal, mystical, speaking of ancient legends and myths – a castle in the sky. The "Sky City" – if you believe the Acoma claim – is the oldest continuously inhabited settlement in the U.S., dating back to the mid 1100's. (Disputed by the Hopi tribe to the northwest, which claims their mesa top village of Old Oraibi predates Acoma.) Coronado's army visited Acoma in 1540 – the first white men to lay eyes on it – and Coronado described it as: "One of the strangest ever seen, because the city was built on a high rock. The ascent was so difficult that we repented climbing to the top... The houses are three and four stories high."

In fact, defense is the most probable reason the Acomas built this village on the sheer-walled island in the sky. In the earliest days ascent was made via hand and toe holds, and ladders which could be pulled up behind them. The Apaches were their arch enemies, before and after the arrival of the Europeans. Intruders were repelled by hurling rocks and boulders down upon them.

But the island-in-the sky wasn't impregnable. In December, 1598, Juan de Zaldivar succeeded in scaling the heights, intent on collecting corn from the pueblo's stores. They were met with fierce resistance, and before it was over Zaldivar and 12 of his men were dead. The Acomas had developed the habit of fierce independence after so many centuries living in their fortress-like home, and didn't bow easily to the demands of intruders. In retaliation Juan de Onate sent a force of 70 men against the Acomas, in a battle which raged for three days. Spanish soldiers outfitted in double strength armor fought Acoma braves in hand-to-hand combat. The Indians, clad in multi-colored blankets, in skins, or naked, wearing masks and face paint, fought bravely. Toward the end the Spanish managed to haul two cannon to the top and laid siege in an even more devastating manner. In the end the swords, muskets and cannon were too much, as many of the Acomas threw themselves into flames or off the sheer cliffs. By some estimates there were more than 600 Acoma dead, with five to six hundred others exiled by the Spanish, many of them to suffer even more retribution later on. For 20 years after that the Acomas were left to peacefully recover and reconstitute their lives in their high village.

The next Spanish invasion was much more peaceable, as Franciscan friar Juan Ramirez succeeded in winning the Acoma's acceptance in 1629. That paved the way for the building of the *San Esteban del Rey Mission,* which was a miracle in itself, as 40 foot timbers, heavy rock, and every other tool and material needed for construction had to be hauled laboriously up the nearly 400 foot high cliffs. But the job was finally accomplished, and the mission completed around 1640. The Pueblo Revolt of 1680 saw another upheaval at Acoma, as many Indians from the Rio Grande Pueblos escaped to Acoma to avoid Spanish retribution. The Spanish did approach the Acoma fortress in 1696 with revenge on their minds, but this time they were content merely to burn the cornfields at the bottom of the cliffs.

## Touring The Pueblos

... Today, a visit to this ancient redoubt finds the place little changed since the old days. The tour starts from the Visitor Center down below (a fee for the tour and for camera use),then up a road to the top aboard a bus. The guide will guide lead you first to the cool interior of the *San Esteban del Rey Mission* with its thick adobe walls and 40 foot ceiling, and to a view of a colorful altar and ceiling painted with ancient Acoma motifs. There's a likeness of St. Stephen painted on a buffalo skin, among other treasures. The tour continues between flat, adobe-walled dwellings reeking

*Acoma "Sky City"*

## Acoma "Sky City"

and beyond. A small, rougher example of Acoma pottery may set you back only a few dollars. Larger vessels of exceptional quality can run into the thousands.

<u>Sightseeing</u> – Inside the Visitor Center there is a tribal museum which includes pottery making displays and historical artifacts and photos. There's a small restaurant too – in a part of the country were eateries are scarce – which serves both Indian and American cuisine. Plenty of gorgeous high desert scenery to be enjoyed throughout the Acoma lands.

<u>Ceremonials</u> – The annual festival is that of *San Estevan Feast Day*, which falls on September 2. Other ceremonials are held at short notice throughout the year.

<u>Bingo</u> – The *Acoma Bingo Parlor* is located on I-40 at Acomita, and is open from noon until 11 PM. Video gambling is located next door to the Bingo room. There's a small cafe next to the video gambling area. For information phone (505) 552-6017.

<u>Ceremonials</u> _ The annual festival is that of *San Estevan Feast Day*, which falls on September 2. Other ceremonials are held at short notice throughout the year.

For more information contact: Acoma Tourist Visitor Center, P.O. Box 309, Acoma NM 87034. Ph. (505) 252-1139 or (800) 747-0181.

*Touring The Pueblos*

## ZUNI

You can reach the Zuni Pueblo by driving south from Gallup, New Mexico, on NM 53. The distance is about 35 miles.

<u>Highlight:</u> *Silver and turquoise jewelry.*

Zuni was the first pueblo to be visited by Spanish explorers back in 1539. It was thought to be one of the legendary "Seven Cities of Cibola" for which the Spaniards searched. A guide named Estevan – an escaped black slave with some rudimentary knowledge of the southwest – was guiding a Franciscan friar named Marcos de Niza through the mountains and deserts of what is now southern New Mexico in 1539, as they searched for the Seven Cities and the gold they were thought to hold. Estevan would keep a few days ahead of the main party and send runners back to de Niza with encouraging words of riches lying just ahead. Estevan – somewhat the rogue, and not averse to taking advantage of the awe in which the Indians seemed to hold him – partook of the fruits of each village, including the women. He finally came to the Zuni enclave, and whether his reputation had

## Touring The Pueblos

preceeded him or not, he was warned to stop short. Of course he failed to follow the advice, and the result was that the Zunis dispatched him forthwith. Fray de Niza, upon hearing of Estevan's death, did stop short of the Zuni Pueblo. But he believed that he had come upon Cibola after all – or was at least willing to advertise that he had done so when he returned to Mexico City and reported to the Viceroy. The report led to Coronado's famous journey of exploration into the southwest the following year. The expedition reached Zuni country after a long and difficult journey. But Coronado was not met with the sight of streets of gold and bejewelled natives as expected. Instead he was besieged by the Zunis first at a place called Bad Pass. Then he became involved in a minor war at a village called Hawikkuh. After a fierce battle (the one and only battle between Zuni and Spaniard), 20 Zuni braves lay dead, with the prospects of even more bloodshed if they continued to fight. The Zunis – a practical people – called it quits for the time being, and an uneasy truce resulted. In fact an uneasy tolerance characterized their relationships with the Spanish from that time forward. The Zunis were friendly to the point of flattery, but never really adopted Spanish ways. Even the various friars who arrived over the years fared poorly, several of them being martyred at the hands of the Indians.

You'll see this same independence of spirit today when you visit this largest of the New Mexico Pueblo tribes. Their individuality can be seen most dramatically in the excellence and variety of their most famous handicraft: *silver and turquoise jewelry.* (Nearby Gallup is the center of the Indian jewelry trade.) It was in 1872 when a Navajo silversmith – Atsidi Chon was his name (sometimes known as Ugly

*Acoma "sky City"*

with antiquity, the sight of shawl-clad cronies taking you back for centuries. The view from the top of this 70 acre city-in-the-sky is marvelous, with Mt. Taylor – often snow capped – visible to the north, and the heights of Enchanted Mesa just to the east. Only a few people continue to live in the old pueblo, the remainder living in the more modern villages of Acomita, McCartys, and Anzac.

As you wend your way along ancient streets you may see examples of another Acoma trademark: distinctive *Acoma pottery*. The claim is that it's the thinnest-walled pottery of all the pueblos, and it may be

*Acoma pottery*

## Touring The Pueblos

true. The vessels are made from what rates as a most stubborn, hard-to-work clay. The dark gray material – gathered locally – must be ground to a powder, soaked, cleaned, and worked laboriously in order to reach a maleable state. Its innate toughness is part of the reason it allows such thin walls. One of its unfortunate characteristics is that it often leaves pitting in the finished surface. When an Acoma potter is successful, however, the result is a treasure. One visual hallmark of this red, white and beige pottery is a razzle-dazzle fine-line design tradition, where cross hatched and geometric patterns are added to clay surfaces, enchanting the eye. Legendary Acoma potter Lucy Lewis was a true master at it. The tradition is based on designs originated by southern New Mexico Mimbres Indians in the 10th and 11th centuries. Also based on Mimbres designs is the emphasis on flower and animal figures, of which the parrot (once common in southern New Mexico) is a traditional favorite. Another common feature is corrugated pottery, where coils of clay (some nearly as thin as spaghetti) are left unsmoothed and even exaggerated to pleasing effect. The pitting problem noted, and the difficulty in preparing the clay, has led some Acoma potters to depart from traditional ways. "Greenware" (already prepared, unfired vessels made by other tribes) is sometimes used, upon which Acoma designs are placed. The kiln firing process is also often employed instead of traditional methods. Best to ask about the extent of these more modern practices before you purchase, if it's important to you.

  Shopping – You can buy pottery items and other Indian-made wares at tables on top of the mesa, at tables in front of the Visitor Center, at a gift shop inside, and at shops and studios across Acoma land

Smith) – traveled to the Zuni Pueblo and moved in with a local resident named Lanyade. The Navajo began teaching the Zuni man the art of silversmithing in return for horses and other goods. By the time he left a year later, Lanyade was proficient enough to create his own silver jewelry, and to pass along the skills to his fellow Zunis. It wasn't until 1890, however, before the Zuni's distinctive approach to jewelry making began to emerge and become known across the southwest and beyond. That was the year they discovered *turquoise*. The sight of turquoise set against silver delighted them to no end. Thus began the Zuni's famous use of semi precious stones in silver settings. It's a trademark that distinguishes Zuni jewelry making to this day. The way

*Zuni Pueblo hornos ovens*

bits of turquoise are worked by Zuni artists to form clusters and rows of silver pieces is a marvel to behold. The working of the stones becomes so fine and intricate at times as to be called "needlepoint." Another class of stonework is the *mosaic*, where stones (coral, jet, shell and others, in addition to turquoise) are arranged in representational and geometric forms in a mind bending variety of rows, clusters, and designs. Each individual stone is formed and cemented into place on a preformed silver base. A similar technique – another trademark feature of Zuni silverworking – is *channel work*, where thin walls of silver are soldered to a base in a broach, pendant, or bracelet, and prefitted stones set exactly into their honeycomb spaces. The surfaces are then ground and polished smooth, leaving a beautiful mosaic, the silver lines setting the stone off to striking effect. You'll find mythological figures (Rainbow Woman, kachina figures), butterflies, foxes, deer, people, landforms, and just about every other animal, mythic, and geographical figure represented in Zuni jewelry. The turquoise stone itself holds an important place in Zuni mythology and religion in and of itself. At first the Zunis practiced their developing art as a sideline, using crude homemade tools, the fruits of their labors enjoyed only by fellow tribe members. But with the opening of the West, more and more tourists became enraptured by Zuni and other Indian jewelry. Silver in the form of sheets and wire became available. New tools such as the gas torch, diamond saw, and carborundum grinding wheels became available, making the use of smaller and smaller stones – a Zuni trademark – feasible and practical. Unlike the Hopi and Navajo approaches to silversmithing, the Zuni approach tends to fill every silver surface with stonework, the silver accenting the

*Zuni*

*Our Lady of Guadalupe Mission
Zuni Pueblo*

stonework instead of the reverse. Eventually the jewelry making craft became an honored, full fledged profession among a large proportion of Zuni families. Out of a total population of about 7,500 Zunis today, fully 1,000 are said to be engaged in the making of Indian arts and crafts. Thus it isn't hard to believe the number of arts and crafts outlets operating in the old Zuni Pueblo. *(Zuni Village Trading Post, Pueblo of Zuni Arts and Crafts., Hawikkuh Trading Post, Running Bear Trading Post,* and others will be found in Zuni Pueblo.)

<u>Sightseeing</u> – For explorers of Zuni Pueblo the crown jewell is probably *Our Lady of Guadalupe Mission Church*, located a couple of blocks south of

*Touring The Pueblos*

NM 53 on Old Mission Way. The mission was completed in 1629, went through a couple of cycles of decay and reconstruction, and then after the most recent refurbishing (in the late 1960's), began to welcome visitors. Hours are 10 AM to Noon; and 1 PM to 4 PM on weekdays. Religious services are still held on Sundays. In the cool interior you'll find religious paintings extending the length of the nave on both sides, and above them the most ambitious set of murals seen in any of the pueblo churchs. The murals – of 24 significant kachina spirits – were begun in 1970 by Zuni artist Alex Seowtewa, the work expected to continue until the mid 1990's. The juxtaposition of Christian and traditional pueblo symbols is one compromise the Catholic faith made early on, in order to encourage attendance. An unusual spiral staircase rises to the choir loft at the right rear of the church. An involuntary hush seems to grip visitors who step into this historical edefice, where the walls are up to eight feet thick. Guided tours of the mission and pueblo lands are available.

Another more recent sightseeing objective is the *Zuni Museum Project*, located on NM 53 just east of the Tribal Administrative Building. The museum is open 9 AM to 4:30 PM on weekdays. The displays will provide good historical background to this first-visited of the New Mexico pueblos.

A walking tour will give some sense of the antiquity of this old village, originally called *Halon:wa* – or "Middle Place" – where, tradition has it, the Zunis were instructed to live after entering this the "fourth world" after exiting the underworld from an opening near the Grand Canyon. The old stone buildings which remain, the dusty streets, the old mission, and the beehive *hornos* ovens help take you back to the old

## Touring The Pueblos

villages with their layered stone dwellings and kivas. If these walls, too, could talk! What resourcefulness and inventiveness and staying power it took to grow crops century after century in this arid, unforgiving land. No wonder that a primary theme in Hopi prayers to the kachina spirits is the call for rain and abundant crops. The old Hopi villages congregate on and around three high mesas (First, Second and Third Mesas), with a sense of history to be found in all of them. There is the village of *Hano*, founded by Rio Grande Tewa speaking Pueblo Indians fleeing from the Spaniards after the Reconquest. To this day Hano remains noticeably separate and distinct from the other Hopi villages – and also separate from their Rio Grande Pueblo ancestors. There is the village of *Old Oraibi* (in contention with Acoma as the oldest continuously inhabited settlement in the U.S.). Seems there was a dispute among the citizens of Old Oraibi at the end of the 1800's regarding the acceptance of mainstream American ways. It threatened to tear the village apart. Before things reached the violent stage, however, it was decided that a *pushing contest* would be held between the believers in the "old ways" and those who wanted to become more modern. (Such recourse to reason and non violence in the settlement of disputes has been a Hopi hallmark through the ages.) The faction which won the pushing contest would be allowed to remain in the village. The losers, on the other hand, would have to find a new place to live. The losing faction ended up founding the village of *New Oraibi*, close by, where they remain today. That oldest of Hopi villages – Old Oraibi – perched on its mesa top, is one of the most fascinating and imagination-stirring of all the villages.

  <u>Sightseeing</u> – Instead of a single historic pueblo village, as with other pueblo villages, the Hopi tribe has

*Hopi*

*Mesa Top Village of Walpi*

*Old Wagon at Moenkopi*

## Touring The Pueblos

Europeans paid no attention to the warning – they weren't accustomed to following the blandishments of North American Indians. The Spanish proceeded to attack the Hopis forthwith, routing them with little effort. But they found no signs of the gold they were seeking here, so after delaying just long enough to make some explorations further west, they departed. The Spanish showed little further interest in this remote, desolate land for almost century. But in 1629 a friar and two priests arrived in a belated attempt to convert the infidel Hopis. The Franciscans built churches and schools at what is now called Old Oraibi, and at Shongopovi and Awatovi, carrying heavy wooden beams all the way from the San Francisco Peaks, 100 miles distant, for use in construction. But the friars had a way of sowing distrust and resentment instead of loyalty and allegiance among the Indians. Friar Perras, especially, earned the Hopi's displeasure – after a promising beginning. Finally the Hopis had enough of Friar Perras, so they martyred him one night, using the venerable poisoning method. Not long after the 1680 Pueblo Revolt, Hopi warriors – dressed in kachina masks – killed all four of the remaining friars and destroyed all three of the mission churches, seemingly wiping their hands once and for all of foreign missionary efforts. But there was one more resurgence of Christianity to come, in the Hopi village of Awatovi. The reconversion of the Awatovis didn't sit well with other Hopi villages, however, so they descended on Awatovi one night and completely destroyed it. The village has never been rebuilt. (The unexcavated ruins are located south of Keams, but are closed to the public.)

One of the charms of a visit to Hopi country is the sense of antiquity you get at sight of the mesa top

## HOPI

One most used route of traveling to the HopiLands is to turn north off I-40 near Holbrook, Arizona, and proceed north on Arizona 77 for about 55 miles until reaching Arizona 264, where you'll turn west. The Hopi lands are located primarily within the bounds of the vast Navajo reservation (largest reservation in the U.S.). The drive is through enchanting painted desert country, with striations of red, orange, lavender and beige shimmering in high desert heat waves. You'll see the high, flat topped mesas on which the historical Hopi villages rest from miles away.

Hopi Highlights: *Picturesque mesa top villages; High quality arts and crafts.*

The Hopi villages had been in existence for centuries by the time 17 mounted Spanish horsemen, a few foot soldiers, and a single Franciscan friar approached the Hopi mesas in the year 1540. Their arrival took the Hopis completely by surprise. They drew a line in the loose sandstone, warning the Spaniards not to proceed further. Of course the

*Touring The Pueblos*

at unscheduled times. Check with tribal offices for dates.

For further information contact: Pueblo of Zuni Tribal Offices, P.O. Box 339, Zuni, NM. 87327. Ph. (505) 782-4481.

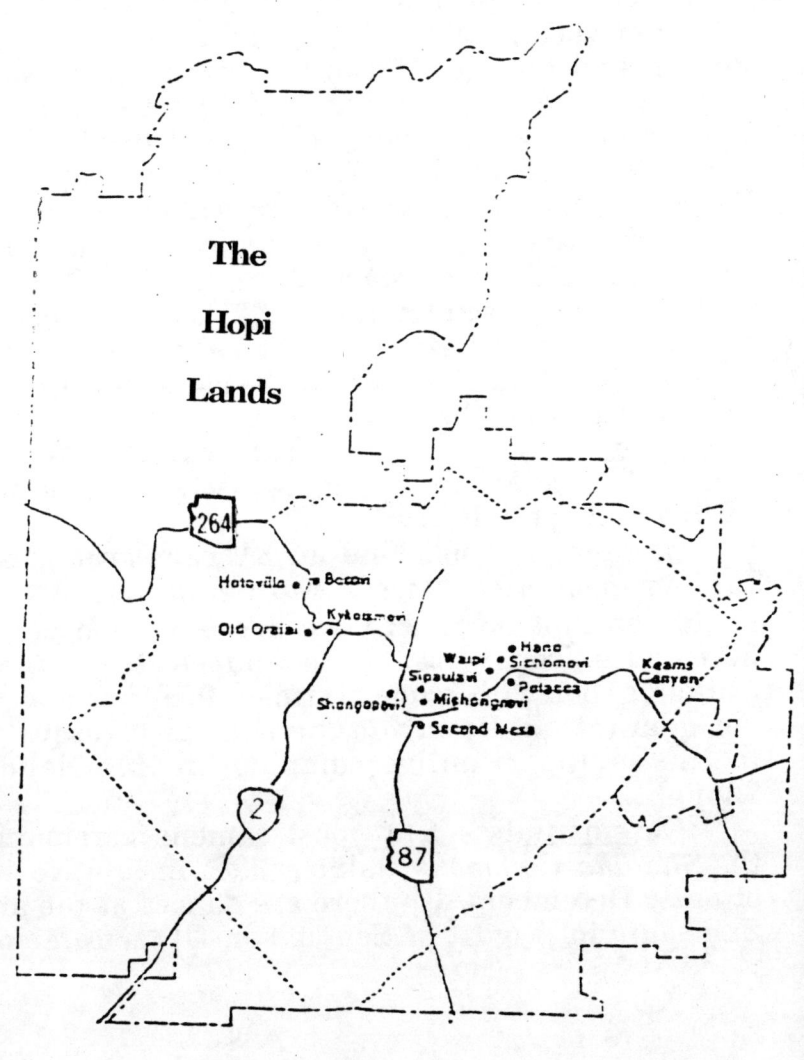

days. Unlike other pueblos, the beehive ovens here tend to be built in clusters, and are interesting subject matter for photographers. (Check on current restrictions regarding photography at the Tribal Administrative Building. No photography within the old mission, and at certain ceremonials.) Just to the east of the village you'll see the flat topped mesa, *Dowa Yalanne,* to the top of which the Zunis have sought refuge at various times before and during the Spanish Period, and during attacks by Apaches and Navajos. This mesa, as with other high retreats in Indian Country, has its mythology of a great flood, when the people escaped to the heights – to the top of Dowa Yallane in this case – to avoid drowning.

<u>Recreation</u> – Fishing for trout and bass at *Ojo Caliente* and *Nutria Lakes.* Fees for non Zunis are: $5/day or $22/season for adults; $2/day or $6/season for juveniles. Hunting also available. Pick up permits at the Fish and Wildlife Office (at the old YACC Building), or at selected merchants.

<u>Food</u> – There are several restaurants in the village. One is *My Place Cafe*, specializing in Indian cuisine and specialty chili.

<u>Camping</u> – You'll find an RV campground at the Zuni town of *Black Mesa,* two miles east of the old pueblo on NM 53. There are a couple of dozen sites here, with iron wheel grills and electrical plug-ins available, but with crude restroom facilities and water not guaranteed. *DowaYalanne* rises picturesquely just to the south. Primitive camping on Zuni lands for $3/night.

<u>Ceremonials</u> – The most famous ceremonial is the *Shalako Ceremony*, taking place in late November or early December. Also there are dances at the annual *Zuni Fair* in August or September. Other ceremonials

## Appendix II

locally crafted wares are offered almost exclusively, and where the seller probably has an intimate knowledge of the items he sells, and the artists who craft them. Next in order is the well proven Indian art retailer who sets high standards and sticks to them. The next category of retailer includes the legion of general gift, curio, department, and other retail stores who may or may not have a high degree of knowledge and integrity when it comes to selling Indian wares. This is where your own expertise will come in most handy in ensuring that you get what you pay for. The retailer who is a member of the *Indian Arts and Crafts Association* (IACA) has sworn to maintain certain high standards in the selling of Indian made wares, so if you see the IACA sticker on a store window, that's a good recommendation. Lowest in reputability might be the Indian made product offered through an ad in the paper, at a flea market, or out of a suitcase. You could get a rare bargain from such a transaction, but chances are better that you won't.

5. Finally, don't hesitate to *ask questions*. The better informed you are, the better your questions will be in determining authenticity and quality. If distinctive pottery is your passion, know at least a few of the basic approaches to potterymaking, and the various design elements, so you can ask probing questions of the seller. If Indian-made jewelry is your interest, it will pay to know such stylistic variations as overlay, inlay, mosaic and channel work, so you can better judge these aspects. If you're considering the purchase of a kachina doll, it would be an advantage to know a little about the kachina making tradition, so as to be able to tell the authentic from the non authentic. For example, a true kachina has a mask on its face. A "kachina" without a mask is not a true kachina, though perhaps still valuable as an Indian crafted doll.

*Touring The Pueblos*

# APPENDIX III

## PUEBLO TOURIST SERVICES

| | FOOD | CAMPING | PHOTOS | FISHING | SHOPPING | TOURS | MUSEUM | BINGO | HIKING |
|---|---|---|---|---|---|---|---|---|---|
| ACOMA | ▶ | | ▶ | ▶ | ▶ | ▶ | ▶ | | |
| COCHITI | | | | ▶ | | | | | |
| HOPI | ▶ | ▶ | ▶ | ▶ | ▶ | ▶ | | | |
| ISLETA | ▶ | ▶ | ▶ | ▶ | ▶ | ▶ | ▶ | | |
| JEMEZ | ▶ | | ▶ | ▶ | | | | | |
| LAGUNA | | ▶ | ▶ | ▶ | | | | ▶ | |
| NAMBE | ▶ | ▶ | ▶ | ▶ | ▶ | ▶ | | | |
| PICURIS | ▶ | ▶ | ▶ | ▶ | | | | | |
| POJOAQUE | | ▶ | | | | | | | |
| SAN FELIPE | | | | ▶ | | | | | |
| SAN ILDEFONSO | ▶ | | ▶ | ▶ | ▶ | ▶ | | | |

## Touring The Pueblos

| | FOOD | CAMPING | PHOTOS | FISHING | SHOPPING | TOURS | MUSEUM | BINGO | HIKING |
|---|---|---|---|---|---|---|---|---|---|
| SAN JUAN | ▶ | | ▶ | ▶ | | | ▶ | | |
| SANDIA | ▶ | | ▶ | ▶ | | | ▶ | ▶ | |
| SANTA ANA | ▶ | | | ▶ | | | | | |
| SANTA CLARA | ▶ | ▶ | ▶ | ▶ | ▶ | | | | |
| SANTO DOMINGO | ▶ | | | ▶ | | ▶ | | | |
| TAOS | ▶ | | | ▶ | | | | | |
| TESUQUE | ▶ | | | ▶ | ▶ | ▶ | ▶ | | |
| ZIA | | | ▶ | ▶ | | | | | |
| ZUNI | ▶ | ▶ | ▶ | ▶ | ▶ | ▶ | | ▶ | |

*Hunting available on some pueblo lands. Check with tribal Fish and Game Departments.

# INDEX

Acoma Pueblo 119-125.
 history, 120,121; Acoma
 pottery, 123,124; shopping
 124,125.
Aguilar Indian Arts Shop 53.
Aguino's Indian Arts and
 Crafts Shop 40.
American Army of the West
 40.
Anasazi Indians 11,43,45.
Arvide, Fray Martin de 31.
Aztec ruins 65.

Bacavi 141.
Bad Pass 128.
Bandalier National
 Monument 49,46.
Bean Dance 146.
Bent, Governor-General
 Charles 26.
Bien Mur Indian Market 102.
Buffalo Dance 86.
Black Mesa 53,133.
Blue Corn 52
Butterfly Balloon Shop 47.

Camel Rock 68,69.
Camel Rock Ranch 69.
Camino Real 80,85,108.
Canyon de Chelly 64.
Castillo de Viejo 34.
Ceremonial wear 87.

Chaco Canyon 64.
Channel work (jewelry
 making) 130.
Children's Museum 147.
Chon, Atsidi 128.
Cloud Eagle Studio
 Gallery 59.
Clown Society Pole Climb 35.
Cochiti Pueblo 73-77; Story-
 teller making 74-76; drum
 making 74,75; recreation,
 ceremonials 76.
Cochiti Lake 78.
Colonel Price 26.
Cordero, Helen 74,99,110.
Corn Studio 47.
Coronado 120,128.
Creations in Clay by Lonnie
 59.

Davis, Jeff 68.
Dowa Yalanne 133.
Dragonfly Recreation Area
 100.
Drums, drum making 74,76,
 87.
Duran's Pottery 69.

Eight Northern Indian
 Pueblos Artist and Craft-
 man Show 40.
Eight Northern Indian

## Touring The Pueblos

Pueblos Council 38,39.
Enchanted Mesa 123.
Estevan 127.

Feast of Our Lady of
  Guadalupe 66.
First Mesa 138-140.
Friar Juan Ramirez 121.
Friar Marcos de Niza 127.
Friar Perras 136.
Frijoles Canyon 74.
Frijoles Falls 56.

Giusewa 95-98.
Green Corn Dance 86.
Greenware 124.
Guttierez Studio 59.

Halon:wa 152.
Hano 138,140.
Hawikkuh 128.
Hawikkuh Trading Post 131.
Heard Museum 75.
Hidden Valley 32.
Hidden Valley Restaurant
  35.
High Country Tri-Cultural
  Arts and Crafts Fair 35.
Hollywood Gate 53.
Holy Ghost Springs Rec-
  reation Area 100.
Hopi Pueblo villages 135-146.
  Jewelry making in 144,145;
  kachina doll making in
  143,144; kachina spirits of
  141; potterymaking in145;
  ceremonials of 146.
Horn Mesa 73.
Hotel Santa Fe 35.

Hotevilla 141.
How To Buy Indian Arts
  And Crafts 149-153.

Indian arts and crafts
  (general) 102,103.
Indian Arts and Crafts
  Association (IACA) 153.
Indian Pueblo Cultural
  Center 147,148.
Isleta Pueblo 107-110.
  potterymaking of 108-
  110; Isleta Lakes 110;
  Isleta Bingo Parlor110.

Jemez Canyon Dam 62.
Jemez Mountains 58.
Jemez Indian Tribe 65.
Jemez Plateau 93.
Jemez Pueblo 95-100.
  fishing in 99,100;
  potterymaking in 99;
  recreation in 99.
Jemez State Monument 98,99.
Juan Tafoya Pottery 53.

Kachina dances 86,146.
Kachina dolls 143. Crafting
  of 143,144.
Kachina spirits 141,152.
Keams Canyon 136.
Kykotsmovi 141.

Lady of Lourdes Chapel 39.
Laguna Pueblo 113-117. crafts
  of 110; recreation in 117;
  St. Joseph Mission Church
  of 114-117.
Lanyade 129.

# Index

Little Feast 110.
Los Cerrillos Turquoise Mine 81.
Lewis, Lucy 124.

Maria Concho's and Crucita's Indian Shop.
Martinez, Julian and Maria 50-52.
Matachina Dances 54.
McCartys 119.
Mera, Dr. Harry.
Merrock Gallerie 47.
Mesa Verde 64.
Micaceous potterymaking 32-34.
Mimbres Indians 52,103,124.
Mishongnovi 140.
Moenkopi 141.
Mogollon Culture 11.
Mosaic daesigns in jewelry 130.
Mt. Taylor 123.
Museum of International Folk Art 75.
My Place Cafe 133.

Nacimiento Mountains 93.
Nambe Pueblo 55-59. Nambe Falls Recreation Area 59; shopping in 58; Nambe Waterfall Ceremonial 58.
Naranjo, Louis and Virginia 76.
Native American Heirlooms 59.
Native Arts Studio 47.
Navajo silversmithing 130.

Needlepoint in Zuni jewelry making 130.
New Mexico state flag symbol, history of 92.
New Mexico camel experiment 67.
New Oraibi 138.
Northern Pueblos Agency 39.
Northern Rio Grande history 56.

O'ke 37.
O'ke Oweenge Arts and Crafts Cooperative 40.
Ojo Caliente Lake 133.
Old Oraibi 136,138.
Ollas 44.
Onate, Juan de 37,95,121.
Oterman, Antonio de 107.
Our Lady of Guadalupe Mission Church 131.

Pajarito Plateau 73,74,93.
Pecos Pueblo 65.
Picuris Pueblo 31-36. micaceous pottermaking in 32-34; Pueblo Enterprises 34-36; recreation in 35.
Pojoaque Pueblo 61-66. Poeh Center 62,63,65; Pojoaque Pueblo Plaza 61; Tourist Center and RV Park 61.
Popay 24,38.
Popovia Da Studio of Indian Arts 52.
Po-Shu ruins 65.
Potsuii pottery style 39.

Prairie Star Restaurant 62.
Pueblo fishing (general) 100.
Pueblo of Zuni Arts and
   Crafts 131.
Pueblo Revolt of 1680 23-25,
   32,53,56,73,95,101,121,136.
Pueblo(general) history
   9-13; pottery, dwellings
   9; setting 11; ceremonials
   15, 86-89; architecture of
   15; people of 17; services
   in 17, Appendix III; arts and
   crafts of 17-18; rules and
   regulations in 18.
Puki 33.
Pu-Na Lake 35.

Reconquest 56,95,113.
Red and black pottery 45.
Red Rock Scenic Area 99.
Refugee pueblo 113.
Reyes Day 54.
Rio Grande bosque 39.
Rio Pueblo 34.
Rio Pueblo de Taos 27.

St. Anthony's Feast Day 101.
St. Augustine Church 108, 110.
St. Buenaventure Feast Day 78.
St. Francis of Assisi Feast Day 59.
St. Jerome Mission Church 28.
St. John's Feast Day 117.
St. Joseph's Feast Day 117.
St. Joseph Mission Church 114-117.

Sandia Mountains 85,101.
Sandia Pueblo 101-105.
   Sandia Lakes Recreation
   Area 103; shopping in 102,
   103; Sandia Trails 104.
San Diego Feast Day 69,100.
San Diego Mesa 95.
San Francisco Peaks 136.
San Felipe Pueblo 75-89.
   ceremonials of 86-89.
San Esteban del Rey Mission 121,122.
San Esteban Feast Day 125.
San Gabriel 37,39.
San Geronimo Feast Day 29.
San Jose de la Jemez 95, 98.
San Jose River 114.
San Juan Pueblo 49-54.
   bingo 41; ceremonials 41;
   Tribal Lakes and Recreation 41; shopping 40.
Sangre de Cristo Mountains 45,53,55.
San Ildefonso Pueblo 49-54.
   potterymaking in 49-51;
   museum in 49; ceremonials of 53.
Santa Ana Mesa 85.
Santa Ana Pueblo 61-66. Ta
   Ya Cooperative
   Association 62.
Santa Clara Pueblo 43-48.
   Puye Cliff Dwellings 43-45;
   potterymaking of 45,46;
   Santa Clara Canyon 45,47;
   shopping, recreation 46,47.
Santa Fe Opera 68.
Santa Fe Indian Market 77.
Santa Fe River 78.

*Hopi*

used to accent and set off the silver rather than the reverse.

A third Hopi craft specialty is that of *potterymaking*. It's been speculated that the legend of the golden vessels which helped launch Coronado's search for the "Seven Cities of Cibola" back in 1540 came from the golden appearance of early Hopi pottery. The Hopi Tribe did have a "golden age" of potterymaking, in the period 1375 to 1625, emanating from the old Sikyatki Pueblo (now in ruins). Sikyatki pottery died out with the abandonment of the pueblo, but was revived again after 1880, using classic designs. Today Hopi pottery is again among the most respected and in demand among the 20 pueblos. It is especially the women in the villages on First Mesa who make the pottery, from yellow and gray clay found in the surrounding area. From these clays come cream, buff, apricot, peach, light red, and yellow vessels, the hue dependant on the firing technique used. And on these clay surfaces are painted all manner of representational and stylized animal, bird, kachina and abstract figure. Fine line scrollwork is one of the trademark features of Hopi pottery, as is the prevalence of broad shouldered, overhanging lips on large bowls, often with additional decorations inside. The same flair for innovation in design is seen in potterymaking as in silver jewelry making.

Lodgings and Camping – Lodgings are available at both Keams Canyon and Shungopavi. Next to the Cultural Center at Shungopavi is a free campground, featuring some picnic tables and grills. Restrooms are available next door at the Cultural Center. No hookups or water, however. For up-to-date restaurant and campground information contact: Hopi Cultural Center, P.O. Box 67, Second Mesa, Arizona. 86043. Ph.

*Touring The Pueblos*

(602) 734-2401/2402. Or, Keams Canyon Motel, P.O. Box 188, Keams Canyon, Arizona. 86034. Ph. (602) 738-2297.

   Ceremonials – Dances are held throughout the year, especially in late spring. In this land of little rain (average about 10 inches/year) the ceremonials dwell especially on petitions for adequate rainfall and good harvests. But much of the supplications of kachina impersonators is for the fostering of peace and goodwill. The Hopis are a people made up of clans, each of which has its own rituals. *Social Dances* are held in January and February. The *Bean Dance* is held in February, with many *kachina dances* held throughout the summer, culminating in the *Niman Dance* in August. The *Snake Dance* (held in alternating Augusts in Shungopavi and Mishongovi) may or may not be open to the public in any given year, so check with the Community Development Offices at these villages for the latest information. In Shungopavi the phone number is (602) 734-2262. For information regarding the First Mesa villages call: ((602) 734-2474. For general information about the Hopi reservation and happenings contact: Office of Public Relations, The Hopi Tribe, P.O. Box 123, Kykotsmovi, AZ 86039. Ph. (602) 734-2441, ext. 341 or 360.

# APPENDIX I

## Indian Pueblo Cultural Center

Anyone interested in the world of the Pueblo Indians should not miss the opportunity of visiting the *Indian Pueblo Cultural Center* in Albuquerque, owned and operated by the 19 New Mexico Pueblos. It's located at 2401 12th Street NW, just one block north of Interstate 40. Downstairs in the main museum section are displays, dioramas, artifacts and other exhibits telling the story of the Puebloans from their beginnings to contemporary times. The visitor will have a good overview of Pueblo historical high points, culture, beliefs and arts and crafts by the time the museum tour is completed.

A new addition to the center is the *Pueblo House Children's Museum* (open 9 AM to 4 PM on Tuesdays, Wednesdays and Fridays, other days by appointment), a unique hands-on facility designed to teach children about Pueblo history and culture.

On the ground level of the Center is a central plaza area where a wide variety of Pueblo cultural events take place throughout the year. Tribal dances, theatrical productions, concerts, workshops, lectures,

*Touring The Pueblos*

and arts and crafts demonstration and fairs are scheduled. Especially during the annual festival (the third week in April) is there a rich array of activities. This week features an even more intensive scheduling of traditional dances, juried arts and crafts exhibits, art lectures, storytelling, an Indian fashion show, sign-ups for tours of Pueblo Country, a *Children's Essay and Poster Contest,* and other events, most of them free to the public. Museum tours are half price during this week only. Unlike many of the pueblos which have limitations regarding photography and sketching, you'll find no such restrictions here.

Surrounding the plaza area on the ground level are shops which display and sell every variety of genuine, authentic Indian arts and craft item. At the north end is a shop area devoted to books specializing in Native American subjects, and travel in the southwest.

At the entrance to the Center is a restaurant serving a large variety of Indian, American and Mexican food. The restaurant is open 7:30 AM to 3:30 PM.

For information and schedules of activities contact: Indian Pueblo Cultural Center, 2401 12th St. NW, Albuquerque NM 87102. Ph. (505) 843-7270, or 800-788-0721.

# Touring The Pueblos

*Hopi Kachinas*

the same complex. Also in the Cultural Center are shops and vendors selling arts and crafts.

Next to the Hopi Cultural Center is the *Hopi Arts and Crafts Silvercrafts Cooperative*, where you'll find the widest range of Hopi silver jewelry and other crafts anywhere on the Hopi reservation. The Cooperative was established in 1949, and continues to foster and promote the efforts of Hopi artists across the country and world. There are other retail establishments selling Hopi wares too, as well as table top and home based sellers, all across HopiLand.

Ten miles west of Second Mesa is *Third Mesa*. Here you'll find the old villages of *Kykotsmovi, Old Oraibi, Hotevilla, Bacavi,* and further to the north, *Moenkopi*. Kykotsmovi is the location of the Hopi tribal offices. Just up the road from Kykotsmovi, perched on the edge of an outcropping of rock, is the aforementioned village of Old Oraibi, dating back to about 1150. Here you'll find the oldest of the old stone dwellings, and the most time worn of foot paths leading off to who knows what field of corn or remote cluster of old dwellings. A smattering of modern housing dilutes the air of antiquity somewhat, but still the sense of time warp is unmistakable and palpable. The Modern Age is still in minimal evidence here, the sense of stoicism and acceptance of harsh realities strong.

One of the chief manifestations of things mystical and traditional in Hopi life is that of the *kachina spirits*. Other pueblos have kachinas too (the Zuni Pueblo, notably) but none hold them so importantly as do the Hopis. In Hopi mysticism the kachinas are the supernatural spirits which embody the basis of Hopi traditional religion. There is *Corn Woman*, who resides beside the *Lake of the Underworld*, and can be likened to the Virgin Mary in spirits is to be represented. Should it be *Kwanitaqa*, the god who guards the gate to the underworld? Should it be an eagle kachina? Or perhaps a black ogre? The imagination and ability of the craftsman takes over as the head is carved, arms installed, outerware fashioned, and very importantly, a mask fabricated and afixed to represent the relevant spirit. The end result is a wooden figurine which is almost always engaging for its unusual accoutrements and visual impact. They're sometimes humorous, often grotesque, but always eye catching.

A second major Hopi craft is *silver jewelry*. The Hopis got a late start in the silver jewelry business (late 1800's), but they've made up for lost time to become ranked with the best of Indian silversmiths. The Hopis are innovative where others often tend toward the cliche. Uneven borderwork in the hands of a mediocre silversmith looks crude, but the better Hopi smiths have a way of making it look even stylish. Two distinguishing characteristics mark the work of Hopi silversmiths: *overlay*, and the emphasis on *silverwork* (as opposed to an emphasis on stone settings which many tribes favor). In overlay the smith starts with a plain sheet of sterling silver (which he may do some imprinting on), then takes another sheet and cuts any of a near infinite variety of artfully shaped openwork designs. This openwork piece is then soldered onto the first piece and the piece treated to blacken it. After the top section is polished to a fine sheen, the openwork is brought into beautiful contrast by the underlying black background. The technique is used widely in bracelets, pendants, hair combs, necklaces, buttons, buckles, and many other jewelry forms. The Hopis do use turquoise, coral and other semi-precious stones – as well as applique and stamping techniques – but they tend to be the way she helps people. There are the *Twin War Gods,* who deal in warfare. There are various ogre kachinas – the ones who keep children in line. It is the kachina spirit pantheon which controls the destinies of individual Hopis (there are more than 260 kachina spirits); which determine how good the harvest will be, determine how much water there will be for irrigation, and how blest with children Hopi couples will be. The kachina spirits reside in places such as a number of sacred mountains (the San Francisco Peaks, near Flagstaff, are sacred to the Hopis). Taking messages to the kachina gods are various masked kachina dancers who perform at ceremonials. In addition to kachina dances, there are *kachina dolls*, to serve as reminders and teaching aids to children and adults.

Arts and crafts – The kachina doll is one of the most distinctive art objects made by Pueblo Indians – especially the Hopis. Originally kachinas were made (much as figurines of Christian saints) for use only by individual Hopis. But when tourists started coming to the southwest, kachinas were discovered to have important commercial possibilities. Nowadays you'll find kachinas for sale everywhere in the southwest and beyond. Kachinas are fascinating and collectable because of the intricateness of their designs, because of their sculptural beauty, and through their religious significance. They aren't mass produced, but made individually by Hopi men, every one different.

A Hopi craftsman begins the making of a kachina by searching out the dead root of a cottonwood tree in some dry wash, and cutting off a piece of suitable size and shape. Traditionally he uses a knife, a sandstone smoothing tool, and other primitive implements to shape the body. At an early point a decision is made regarding which of the many kachina

*Indian Pueblo Cultural Center mural by Philbert Hughte of Zuni Pueblo.*

# Index

Santo Domingo Pueblo 75, 79-83. Arts and Crafts Market 82; Cultural Center 82; Corn Dances 83; Heishe necklaces 102; Indian Trading Post 81,82.
School of American Research 93.
Second Mesa 138-140.
Seowtewa, Alex, 132.
Seven Cities of Gold 127.
Shalako Ceremony 86, 133.
Shungopavi 136,140.
Sikyatki Pueblo 145.
Singing Water Pottery and Tours 47.
Sipaulovi 140.
Snake Dances 146.
Social Dances 146.
Storyteller figures 74-76.

Ta Ya Cooperative Association 62.
Tableta Dances 86.
Taos Pueblo 23-30. Battle of 1847 26; pow wow 29; San Geronimo Feast Day 29; Taos Indian Horse Ranch 29.
Tapatu, Luis 32.
Teller, Stella 109.
Teresa Tapia Pottery 69.
Tesuque Pueblo 67-70. recreation, shopping in 69.
Tewa Indian Restaurant 40.
Third Mesa 138-140.
Toni Roller Pottery and Green Leaves Studio 47.
Toreva 140.
Torres Indian Arts 53.
Towa Arts and Crafts Show 99.
Tsankawi Ruins 50-51.
Tunyon Mesa 49
Tyuonyi 64

Valle Grande Golf Course 62
de Vargas, Diego 73,95

Walpi 140

# APPENDIX II

## How To Buy
## Indian Arts and Crafts

It will pay the shopper to be clear about what is high quality and what is not high quality when purchasing handmade Indian arts and crafts. For example, the highest standard in a silver and turquoise bracelet should ideally have a design that is original and unique, with the silver content indeed sterling silver (consisting of 92.5% silver and 7.5% copper or other metal); The piece should be handmade according to an accepted definition (it's legitimate to use such modern innovations as powered drills); the turquoise should be high grade, number one natural turquoise; the craftmanship should be high; and finally, the piece – by definition – should be handmade by a Native American craftperson (with perhaps a second pair of hands legitimately assisting). At the other extreme of quality is the bracelet in which the silver is not sterling at all (and may even be nickel silver); the design not original and unique (and possibly one of perhaps thousands made on an assembly line using mass techniques such as spin casting); the turquoise may not be turquoise at all, but a substitute such as dyed plastic;

and the work maybe not done by Native Americans at all, or maybe not even by Americans.

From a practical standpoint, most buyers can't afford to buy that idealized highest quality silver and turquoise bracelet described. But there are alternatives which still provide the essence of quality Indian handcrafted jewelry, but at a more affordable price. Top quality turquoise (the dwindling supply mined mostly in Persia and the American Southwest these days) has become very expensive, as have such traditional setting materials as coral. But certain legitimate manipulations are widely used to make turquoise more affordable, while retaining essential longlasting beauty and durability. A technique call "stabilization" is legitimately employed to make lower grade turquoise achieve the hardness and longlasting beauty of the very expensive kind, via the injection of polymer plastics or sodium sillica gel. But where turquoise becomes "treated" with various mineral and petroleum solutions to temporarily enhance the color and hardness, the result can actually be a reduction in beauty and preservation over time. The key question is: how has the turquoise been manipulated, if at all? No harm in buying manipulated turquoise so long as you know how it has been manipulated, and if you don't end up paying for a higher grade. Turquoise is also regularly "reconstituted," where fragments are cemented together and reshaped. The cheapest "turquoise"of all is the turquoise substitute, made from look-alike dyed quartz or plastic. Pity the buyer who pays a premium price for these lower grades.

Silver is the other basic material used in Indian jewelry, and here it is in the content of the silver, and the working of it where the purchaser may not be getting his money's worth. There are simple tests to

*Appendix II*

determine silver content if there is reason to doubt the "sterling silver" claim.

In the actual crafting of the jewelry, the departures from "handmade by Indians" can be many and diverse. The ideal is where the Indian silversmith produces original work by his own hand. One step removed is where several Native American craft persons work together, each doing specialized tasks (soldering, polishing, etc.). Further removed from the ideal is where machines are employed for shaping (spin casting is one way) of traditional designs, with Native Americans perhaps running the machines. Finally there is the domestic or foreign made product, the only thing "Indian" about it being the traditional "Indian style" that was perhaps copied from an original Indian design. Nothing wrong with purchasing any of these alternatives, of course, so long as you know what you're buying, pay a fitting price, and aren't especially interested in the authenticity aspect.

A buyer can also be deceived when it comes to buying Indian handmade pottery. Is that pot really completely handmade by a Native American, using traditional methods, designs and materials, as advertised? Or were pottery wheels, electric kilns, commercial clays and paints used instead, possibly by non Indian craftpersons? Again, nothing wrong with buying pottery that was made by non traditional means (some Acoma potters use greenware, kiln baking, and commercial paints, as do some potters from other pueblos). The question is that of misrepresentation. The buyer has the right to know how authentically handmade a pot is, and the authenticity of the "Indian made" label.

Misrepresentations are often made concerning

other types of Indian wares too. How can the buyer protect himself and get what he pays for?

1. *Become familiar with the variety of Indian made craft which captures your fancy.* For example, there are slight differences between sand cast silver products (the hand crafting method) and spin cast (the method used in mass production). With an educated eye you can usually tell the difference. If you know what you're looking for in turquoise you can usually (but not always) tell the difference between genuine turquoise and turquoise substitutes. A number of excellent books are available which discuss the finer points of genuine Indian arts and crafts.

2. Having *an educated eye* will have the additional effect of refining your taste, enabling you to better know what really appeals to you. Pleasing yourself is, after all, the ultimate goal. Nothing at all wrong with buying lower grade items so long as you know them for what they are, and are happy with the product.

3. Even if you have an educated eye, however, and know what you like, it's still easy to become fooled when it comes to judging quality and authenticity. Even the experts are fooled at times. That's why it pays to *buy from reputable dealers.* The factor of trust is an important one in a mass market society in which the artist is rarely known to the buyer. Perhaps the most reputable of all dealers would be the Indian artist him or herself, who you find at a workbench on a reservation or at an Indian market. You can count on the item being authentic then, and the answers to your questions regarding crafting methods probably honest. There is an additional pleasure from buying directly from the artist who created the piece. Almost as reputable is the reservation store or trading post, where

*Hopi*

*Stone dwellings at Old Oraibi.*

12 such, clustered atop and just below First, Second and Third Mesas. The Hopis moved to the mesa tops especially after the Navajos and Apaches (their chief enemies in the old days) adopted the horse from the Spanish, enabling them to increase the scale of their raiding activities. It is these mesa top villages which provide visitors with a unique sense of timelessness and antiquity, and a unique sense of history. Ancient stone buildings perch at the edges of cliffs. Wooden ladders jut up from below-ground kiva spaces where medicine men disseminate information passed on through countless generations. Old men and women with the wisdom of the ages on their faces sit under thatched awnings, looking out over a vast surrounding

## Touring The Pueblos

space of flatlands, punctuated here and there by sculpted buttes and mesas rising abruptly from the mottled desert floor. You'll see artisans – young and old – presenting pottery, silver jewelry, kachinas, baskets and other items for sale. The Hopi lands were the most remote from the early Spanish influence, so you'll find few of the Spanish *horno* ovens here, and no old Spanish missions.

Atop First Mesa You'll find what is perhaps the most colorful of the Hopi villages – that of *Walpi*, at the west end of the mesa. Colorful because of its cliff edge location, and picturesque buildings. It can be visited by taking one of the regular walking tours offered by local guides. (Check in at the Visitor Center at Sichomovi, the middle village on this mesa top.) The guide will provide a world of fascinating information regarding local history and sights. Unfortunately for photo buffs, the traditional Hopi need for privacy mandates that no photos be taken of this very photogenic village. At the eastern end of this high mesa is *Hano-Tewa,* the village established after the Pueblo Revolt by Tewa peoples from along the Rio Grande. This little village managed to keep its old Tewa culture and language alive, surrounded as it is by Hopi influences. At the bottom of First Mesa is the more modern village of *Polacca,* with its up-to-date dwellings and businesses.

Ten miles to the west, across flat, high desert landscape scattered with pinon, juniper, sage and grasslands is Second Mesa. Here you'll find the mesa top villages of *Shungopavi, Sipaulovi* and *Mishongnovi*, with the tiny village of *Toreva* at the west foot. At Shungopavi is where you'll find the *Hopi Cultural Center*, which includes a museum (open Mon-Fri 8 AM to 5 PM; weekends from 9 AM to 2 PM. Adults $3, kids $1.) A restaurant (open 7 AM-9PM) is located in